Sex and Relationships Education

A Step-by-Step Guide for Teachers

Simon Blake

David Fulton Publishers
London

SEX
EDUCATION
FORUM

David Fulton Publishers Ltd
The Chiswick Centre, 414 Chiswick High Road, London W4 5TF

www.fultonpublishers.co.uk

First published 2002
Reprinted twice 2003
10 9 8 7 6 5 4 3

Copyright © Simon Blake 2002

British Library Cataloguing in Publication Data
A catalogue record for this book is available from the British Library.

ISBN 1–85346–834–7

Typeset by Elite Typesetting Techniques Ltd., Eastleigh, Hampshire, UK
Printed and bound in Great Britain by The Thanet Press, Margate

Contents

About the Sex Education Forum

The Sex Education Forum is the national authority on sex and relationships education. Based at the National Children's Bureau, the Forum is a consensus-making umbrella body with 50 member organisations from religious, health, education, children's, parenting and specialist organisations who work together to improve sex and relationships education for all children and young people in different settings. The Forum was established in 1987. The Forum works to improve the climate for sex and relationships education through policy and media work and runs projects to develop best practice. Findings are disseminated to the field through a range of practical factsheets and publications, as well as a termly newsletter *Sex Education Matters*.

All of our work is collaborative, working with members and local and national colleagues to draw together and share information on policy and practice. For further information, please contact us at 8 Wakley Street, London, EC1V 7QE or email sexedforum@ncb.org.uk or visit the website www.ncb.org.uk/sef

Acknowledgements

The Sex Education Forum always works closely with local and national colleagues. Directly and indirectly the creativity, ideas and vision of literally hundreds of people over many years are reflected here. This guide to sex and relationships education is full of ideas and strategies developed by members and colleagues since the Forum's inception in 1987. There are too many people to name – but to all of you, you know who you are, thank you.

In particular the following people have contributed material for this publication. Thank you to Caroline Ray, Sarah Thistle and Janine Jolly for their contribution to the primary school chapter, Ruth Hilton and Lorraine King to the Pupil Referral Unit chapter and Lorna Scott and Lesley Kerr Edwards to the chapter on children and young people with learning disabilities. John Rees contributed to the section on peer education. Sue Plant contributed the section on the organisation of SRE in secondary schools. Paula Power contributed to the section on curriculum planning and assessment in Chapter 3 and commented on the draft publication. Thank you to everyone who contributed or gave permission to use case studies, particularly to Dot Kesterton from King Edward VII School in Sheffield, Teresa Nash, Senior Lecturer/Sexual Health Nurse, Kingston University and St George's Hospital Medical School and Gill Morris and the Camden Healthy Schools Team for permission to adapt the audit tool on pp. 116–117.

Thanks to Helen Chenaf and Tracey Anderson for administrative support. Thanks to Gill Frances for generous support, ideas and thinking and for commenting on the draft publication.

Finally, thanks to all the children and young people, including NCB Young Members, for talking to us about sex and relationships education. I hope this resource reflects their views and ideas. As one boy said, *'After all, we are the next generation, we have to get it right!'*

Simon Blake
April 2002

Introduction

They [children and young people] have to learn that it is not a subject to be scared of.
They need to learn about feelings, relationships, sex, diseases, the whole lot.
(young man aged 15)

Sex and relationships education (SRE) is an educational entitlement for children and young people and must build upon the best available evidence as to what works. It should support children and young people in managing puberty and adolescence and prepare them for an adult life in which they can:

- Be aware of and enjoy their sexuality.
- Develop positive values and a moral framework that will guide their decisions, judgements and behaviour.
- Have the confidence and self-esteem to value themselves and others.
- Behave responsibly within sexual and personal relationships.
- Communicate effectively.
- Have sufficient information and skills to protect themselves and their partner from unintended/unwanted conceptions and sexually transmitted infections including HIV.
- Neither exploit others nor be exploited.
- Access confidential advice and support.

(Sex Education Forum 1999)

The context for SRE has greatly improved in recent years in England. A national and local infrastructure has developed through the National Healthy School Standard and the Teenage Pregnancy Strategy. Personal, Social and Health Education (PSHE) and Citizenship frameworks were published as part of the National Curriculum (QCA/DfEE 1999) supported by additional guidance on SRE (DfEE 0116/2000). Ofsted has produced a good practice report on SRE (Ofsted 2002) and inspectors will be trained to inspect SRE in schools. The DfES and the DH are working with the National Healthy School Standard to pilot an accreditation process for the teaching of PSHE.

This book has been written for teachers to help develop SRE as part of PSHE and Citizenship. It offers:

- a definition of PSHE and Citizenship;
- an overview of the law, national policy, guidance and initiatives and principles of good practice that are applicable across different settings;
- a process for developing a policy and values framework;
- an overview of effective learning methods and an explanation of how groups work;
- an exploration of the needs of particular groups of children and young people;
- advice on working in primary schools;
- advice on working in secondary schools;
- advice on working with children with learning disabilities;
- advice on working in Pupil Referral Units;
- advice on providing professional development activities that can be done alone or in groups;
- a glossary of terms that often arise in sex and relationships education;
- an audit tool.

1 What is PSHE and Citizenship?

PSHE and Citizenship is the planned provision for personal and social development. It helps children and young people develop a secure sense of identity and helps them to function well in the world (SEF 2001). PSHE and Citizenship includes three elements:

- the acquisition of accessible, relevant and age-appropriate information;
- clarification and development of attitudes and values that support self-esteem and are positive to health and well-being;
- the development of personal and social skills to enable emotional development and interaction with others as well as making positive health choices and actively participating in society.

Effective PSHE and Citizenship underpins learning and can contribute significantly to school improvement. It is provided across the curriculum in all subject areas as well as in planned programmes of PSHE and Citizenship. It includes areas such as emotional health and well-being, sex and relationships, drugs, citizenship and careers/vocational education, diet and exercise and safety. School-based PSHE and Citizenship complements and helps children and young people make sense of what is implicitly or explicitly learnt at home from parents, carers, family, friends and the wider society.

Children and young people need an integrated provision of PSHE and Citizenship. Often there is a tendency to focus on specific topics; advocates of specific topics such as sex and relationships and drugs demand more time and more guidance. Approaching PSHE in this topic-based fashion means there is a tendency to focus on information provision and ignore the co-ordinated skills development and values exploration that underpin all personal and social development work (Blake and Frances 2001).

The Sex Education Forum believes that all SRE should be delivered within a safe and supportive environment, and within the broad context of PSHE and Citizenship.

What is SRE?

SRE is a lifelong process of acquiring information, developing skills and forming positive beliefs and attitudes about sex, sexuality, relationships and feelings (Sex Education Forum 1999). SRE (as part of PSHE and Citizenship) should support positive levels of self-esteem and the development of emotional resourcefulness in children and young people. Self-esteem is the way that we feel about ourselves. It is not static; our self-esteem varies throughout our lives depending on circumstances and events. Emotional resourcefulness is the ability to:

- use our thinking skills together with our emotions to guide our behaviour positively;
- manage and respond to negative life events effectively.

Who is SRE for?

SRE is for all children and young people. Development of policy and practice should take into account the needs of boys as well as girls, those who are lesbian, gay, bisexual and heterosexual, those with physical, learning or emotional difficulties and those with a religious, faith or cultural tradition (Sex Education Forum 1999).

Children's and young people's participation underpins all SRE work. To ensure that it meets their needs, they need to participate in the planning and delivery of SRE. We need to find out from them what they want and need to know. This will help to ensure that it meets the needs of ALL children and young people and be relevant to their needs. As one young woman said, '*I think that it is completely wrong that you [adults] think you have the right to tell us what we want to hear. Why don't you find out what we want to know about?*' If we engage effectively with children and young people, it is likely that we are going to meet their needs and address their concerns.

Why is SRE in schools important?

Children and young people tell us that they want to learn about relationships, sex and sexuality

They are particularly keen to develop emotional and social skills necessary for decision-making, negotiating and developing friendships and relationships and to explore 'real-life dilemmas' (Sex Education Forum 2000). For some children, particularly boys and those from black and minority ethnic communities, schools may be their main source of information about sex and relationships (Holland 1994; Lenderyou and Ray 1997).

4

For many children and young people, sex and relationships education:

- Begins too late – often after they have started puberty, have experienced sexual feelings and sexual attraction and often after they have begun sexual activity.
- Has an inadequate amount of time allocated to it and therefore does not cover the wide range of issues including skill development and attitude clarification; instead it focuses on the information elements.
- Is too biological in nature – so the emphasis often lies in reproduction and biology and SRE does not provide adequate time to think about emotions, relationships and 'dilemmas'. *'Schools give a more technical opinion rather than an emotional one and when you are actually going through a situation to do with sex or relationships, it is more to do with emotions'* (young woman, aged 14).
- Is not taken seriously enough by teachers and so pupils do not take it seriously either. This means they do not get the learning opportunities they want.

'Sometimes the teachers are not organised and they just say, do this worksheet, it is not fair' (boy aged 10). 'They don't seem to want to do it, it is not what they are interested in, so we just bunk it or talk at the back, we don't take it seriously' (young woman, aged 15).

Children and young people have many good ideas about how to improve SRE in their school and we should offer structured opportunities to obtain their views. This can ensure that teachers and pupils work together to review and further develop the SRE curriculum. As one young woman, aged 14, said, *'It needs to be of the time, and so we need to be involved in making decisions about what is covered.'*

Parents want schools to do it

In the most recent large-scale study in this country over 94 per cent of parents support school-based SRE, and this is confirmed by smaller-scale studies (HEA/NFER 1994). Less than 1 per cent withdraw their children from sex and relationships education (Ofsted 2002).

Although parents often want to talk to their children about sex and relationships, they feel ill equipped to do so and therefore look to schools to either partially or completely do the job (Dix 1996). *'Some parents feel uncomfortable talking about it with their child and some just leave it to the school to do, which does not really work'* (young man, aged 12).

SRE supports learning

Early findings from the National Healthy School Standard suggest that PSHE and Citizenship developed within the context of a healthy school positively affects achievement across the curriculum, improves behaviour and reduces truancy (Rivers *et al.* 2000).

It is a legal requirement for schools to provide SRE

The National Curriculum (QCA/DfEE 1999) is underpinned by a stated belief in education, at home and at school, as a route to the spiritual, social, cultural, physical and moral development, and thus the well-being, of the individual. It has two broad aims that provide an essential context within which schools can develop their own curriculum:

1. The school curriculum should aim to provide opportunities for all pupils to learn.
2. The school curriculum should aim to promote pupils' spiritual, moral, social and cultural development and should prepare all pupils for the opportunities and responsibilities of life.

In summary, these aims ensure that the curriculum enables pupils to develop the knowledge and understanding of their own and different beliefs in an equal opportunities framework. Pupils will be able to understand their rights and responsibilities, and will develop enduring values and integrity and autonomy and respect for their environment and their communities. SRE promotes pupils' self-esteem and emotional development and helps them form and maintain satisfying relationships.

PSHE and Citizenship are central to achieving these aims. The National Curriculum offers a non-statutory framework for PSHE and Citizenship that is delivered through four strands at all Key Stages. These are:

*   developing confidence and responsibility and making the most of their abilities;
*   preparing to play an active role as citizens;
*   developing a healthier, safer lifestyle;
*   developing good relationships and respecting the differences between people.

In addition, Citizenship has a statutory status at Key Stages 3 and 4 and is delivered through three further strands:

*   knowledge and understanding of becoming informed citizens;
*   developing skills of enquiry and communication;
*   developing skills of participation and responsible action.

SRE is an integral part of PSHE and Citizenship. The *Sex and Relationship Education Guidance* (DfEE 0116/2000) is supported in legislation by the Learning and Skills Act (2000). This requires that young people:

*   learn about the nature and importance of marriage for family life and the bringing up of children; and
*   are protected from teaching and materials that are inappropriate with regard to the age and the religious and cultural background of the pupils concerned.

The Education Act (1996) consolidated all relevant previous legislation and is supported by the SRE *Guidance* (DfEE 0116/2000).

6

In summary;

- SRE should contribute to preparing pupils for the 'opportunities, responsibilities and experiences of adult life' and schools should 'take such steps as are reasonably practical to secure that where SRE is given to any registered pupil it is given in such a manner as to encourage those pupils to have due regard to moral considerations and the value of family life'.
- The sex education elements contained in the National Curriculum Science Orders are mandatory for all pupils of primary and secondary age. This covers anatomy, puberty and biological aspects of sexual reproduction.
- All schools must provide an up-to-date policy that describes the content and organisation of SRE provided outside the National Curriculum Science Order. It is the school governors' responsibility to ensure that the policy is developed and made available to parents for inspection. The DfEE *Guidance* on SRE suggests that schools should have an overall PSHE and Citizenship policy that includes SRE. The policy should complement other policies such as equal opportunities and confidentiality.
- Primary schools should have a policy statement that describes the SRE provided, or gives a statement of the decision not to provide SRE other than that provided within the National Curriculum. The SRE *Guidance* strongly recommends that all primary schools provide sex and relationships education, and that it starts *before* children begin puberty.
- Secondary schools are required to provide an SRE programme that includes (as a minimum) information about sexually transmitted infections and HIV/AIDS.
- Special schools may need to make separate arrangements for primary-aged children and secondary-aged children. The SRE *Guidance* states that both mainstream schools and special schools have a duty to ensure that children with special educational needs and learning difficulties are properly included in SRE.
- Pupil Referral Units have a duty to provide SRE. DfEE Circular (11/99 Social Inclusion, point 6.23) states: 'PRUs teaching pupils of secondary age must provide sex education. If children of primary age are admitted, the teacher in charge must consider whether to offer sex education. The teacher must have a written statement of policy on the content and organisation of sex education, or, if sex education is not part of the curriculum, of that decision. The LEA must ensure that it encourages pupils to have due regard to moral considerations and the value of family life.'
- Parents have the right to withdraw their children from any SRE that is provided outside the National Curriculum Science Orders. However, they cannot withdraw their children from National Curriculum subjects. The SRE *Guidance* emphasises the importance of consultation with parents and members of the wider community to build their confidence in SRE. Approximately four in every ten thousand children are withdrawn from SRE (Ofsted 2002). The Department for Education and Skills provides a leaflet for parents who withdraw their children from SRE. It is available by phoning DfES publications – 0845 602 2260 quoting reference code DfES 0706/2001 or visiting www.dfes.gov.uk/sreandparents.
- Section 28 of the Local Government Act does not prevent the discussion of homosexuality in schools. The SRE *Guidance* states: 'all pupils, whatever their

developing sexuality, need to feel that SRE is relevant to them and sensitive to their needs' (2000: 12).

Ofsted inspectors evaluate PSHE and Citizenship

There is an increasing emphasis on the inspection of PSHE and Citizenship and inspectors are now being trained to inspect SRE. Inspection will take place through:

- examples of achievement and teaching;
- judgement of standards in each of the strands;
- judgement of provision in each of the strands;
- commenting on the management and implementation of PSHE and Citizenship.

Ofsted have also undertaken a survey of good practice in sex and relationships education to demonstrate what can be achieved. A report, *Sex and Relationships*, will be circulated to all schools in 2002. Ofsted is placing more emphasis on the importance of children and young people participating in the development of PSHE and Citizenship.

SRE contributes to the reduction of teenage pregnancy and improving sexual health

The UK has the highest teenage pregnancy rates in Western Europe. In 1998 95,000 young women became pregnant in England. Almost 8000 of these young women were under 16 (ONS 1999). There is a ten-year strategy to reduce teenage pregnancy by 50 per cent (Social Exclusion Unit 1999). This outlines three key reasons for the high teenage pregnancy rates in England. These are:

- mixed messages;
- ignorance;
- low expectations.

There is also a sexual health and HIV strategy which aims to address the poor sexual health of the nation, particularly that of marginalised and vulnerable children and young people.

Some facts about the sexual health of young people:

- Research in Scotland found that out of over 7000 13 and 14 year olds, 18 per cent of boys and 15.4 per cent of girls reported that they had had heterosexual intercourse. Of these, 27 per cent of the boys and 32 per cent of the girls said that they felt that this had been too early. More regret was expressed by boys who had exerted pressure on girls and by girls who felt pressurised into having sex (Wight *et al.* 2000);
- Between 1998 and 1999 cases of gonorrhoea rose by 39 per cent among young men aged between 16 and 19, and by 24 per cent among women of the same age. Chlamydia rates rose by 23 per cent in young men aged between 16 and 19, and by 20 per cent in young women (PHLS 2000);

- HIV infection rates have risen significantly among young people aged 16–19 years (PHLS 2000).

There is increasing evidence that SRE that meets certain requirements can contribute to a reduction in teenage pregnancy rates. Teenage pregnancy is a complex public health issue. Many people look to SRE to reduce teenage pregnancy or use teenage pregnancy rates as a measure of the effectiveness of SRE, but this is not realistic (Blake and Frances 2001). However, there is a growing body of evidence that suggests a broad-based sex and relationships education programme, well linked to contraceptive and sexual health services, can contribute to a reduction in teenage pregnancy rates.

Effective SRE:

- is provided early – before puberty, before feelings of sexual attraction and before young people develop sexual relationships ;
- is empowering for ALL pupils, regardless of sexuality, gender, ethnicity, faith, ability or disability;
- offers a positive and open view of sex and sexuality and supports sexual self-acceptance;
- is both a mainstream entitlement and is targeted at children and young people who may be particularly vulnerable to poor sexual health such as those in care;
- is linked to sexual health services;
- meets specific 'local' needs and trends;
- ensures that pupils and teachers:

  - know what they are doing;
  - why they are doing it;
  - how they are going to do it;
  - how they will know if they have achieved their aims;

- reinforces value messages;
- focuses on risk reduction;
- uses active learning methods and participatory techniques;
- ensures that children and young people develop a critical awareness of messages about sex in the media.

(Health Development Agency 2001)

2 A whole-school approach to SRE

This chapter discusses the National Healthy School Standard (NHSS) criteria for a whole-school approach in relation to SRE. These criteria are laid out in their document *Guidance* (1999).

The National Healthy School Standard

The National Healthy School Standard outlines the importance of a whole-school approach to children's and young people's personal, social development. Children and young people learn about sex and relationships from all sorts of places, not just in formal SRE lessons. They learn by observation and through their experience of the way in which adults and pupils behave. They learn by watching what is and is not acceptable behaviour and by the type of activities and interests in which boys and girls are encouraged to participate.

The school environment and the school ethos support and reflect the positive messages about sex and relationships that are offered within SRE. Children and young people need to see adults modelling positive relationships and respect for diversity.

Working towards becoming a healthy school through a local healthy schools programme or using the principles and criteria set out within the National Standard will help managers, PSHE co-ordinators, teachers and pupils plan together to develop a positive ethos as well as plan and deliver high-quality SRE. The NHSS is a national programme with a regional and local network. Every LEA has developed a local programme with health and other partners. The local programme offers training, support and an accreditation process for schools. A healthy school provides an environment in which children and young people can do 'their best'. The NHSS stresses the importance of diversity and equality issues and provides a robust and flexible framework within which local areas and schools can respond to the specific needs of their pupils.

Healthy schools work with pupils, parents and staff as well as other members of the school community to develop activities that will support both the raising of education standards and improvements in health. This is done both within the formal curriculum and within the general ethos and climate of the school.

11

As well as the criteria for the whole-school approach, there are eight key themes of the NHSS, one of which is SRE. The criteria for SRE reflect the evidence base, national guidance and good practice. They are as follows:

- The school has a policy which is owned and implemented by all members of the school including parents and pupils and is delivered in partnership with local health and support services.
- The school has a planned SRE programme (including information, social skills development and values clarification) which identifies learning outcomes, appropriate to pupils' age, ability, gender and level of maturity and which is based on pupils' needs assessment and a knowledge of vulnerable pupils.
- Staff have a sound basic knowledge of SRE issues and are confident in their skills to teach sex education and discuss sex and relationships.
- Staff have an understanding of the role of schools in contributing to the reduction in teenage conceptions and the promotion of sexual health.

Further information can be found in the National Healthy School Standard documents *Guidance* and *Getting Started* (1999), available by visiting the Wired for Health website – www.wiredforhealth.co.uk – or by contacting the national team based at the Health Development Agency (see Useful organisations p. 125).

Leadership, management and managing change

PSHE and Citizenship often fails to receive adequate resourcing and priority within the school curriculum. Children and young people are acutely aware when teachers do not take it seriously and therefore they do not take it seriously themselves. For it to be considered important by both staff and pupils, there is a need for clear leadership from the Senior Management Team (SMT) and full governor support.

SRE will be most successful if the SMT recognises the role of personal, social development in school improvement and SRE gains a place on the school development or school improvement plan. Securing this type of support will ensure effective planning and adequate timetable space as well as professional development opportunities for staff involved in the delivery of SRE.

A named co-ordinator with clearly defined roles and responsibilities will help in the planning and delivery of SRE. Ofsted recommends that all secondary schools establish specialist teams so that the quality of teaching and coherence is improved (Ofsted 2002). Further information about the organisation and planning involved in the development of specialist teams in secondary schools is given on pp. 72–3.

Target setting

When working towards improving SRE as part of a whole-school approach to becoming a healthy school it is important to audit existing provision to identify what is already being done well and to review areas for further development. To be helpful, targets need to be SMART: Specific, Measurable, Achievable, Realistic and

Time-related. Targets may be in terms of policy and practice development or in terms of the whole-school ethos. Ultimately whatever the target, the end result should be improved pupil learning in SRE.

Targets need to be supported by a process and action plan. So, for example, a specific target may be 'to improve pupils' awareness of local community sexual health services and their skills in accessing help and support'. To achieve this, a number of steps will need to be taken including:

- Developing baseline data against which success can be measured – how many pupils know about community services and feel confident in accessing them?
- Reviewing the whole-school ethos – do we as a school encourage pupils to access help and support and recognise this as a positive quality?
- Review of policy:

  - Do we advertise local community services? Do we need to review the policy framework to enable this to happen?
  - Are staff clear that it is acceptable to inform pupils of community services?
  - Do we involve staff from community services in the delivery of the programme?
  - Do visits to services in the community form part of SRE?

By asking questions such as these, a plan of action can be developed to meet the target.

The four cornerstones of effective SRE development

The four cornerstones of effective policy and practice development are:

1. Participation of children and young people.
2. Partnership with parents, carers and the wider community.
3. Policy development.
4. Practice (curriculum) development.

Figure 2.1 presents details of the four cornerstones of effective SRE.

Policy development

All policies should be developed in line with legal requirements and non-statutory guidance. Ofsted (2002) found that the (new) guidance from the DfEE has had a significant impact, with many schools revising their policies to reflect the new guidance. It recommends that schools have an overall PSHE and Citizenship policy of which SRE will be a discrete part. It emphasises that for many pupils school-based SRE will be their main source of accurate information and education about sex and relationships. It highlights the importance of policies that are both 'culturally appropriate and inclusive of all children', and emphasises that:

The Four Cornerstones of Effective SRE

All SRE needs to be developed in the context of PSHE and Citizenship and a whole-school ethos that is safe for children and young people to learn in and supports their self-esteem and emotional development.

Participation

For SRE to be relevant to the pupils they should be engaged in the policy and practice development. There are a range of ways that pupils can be involved.

✓ As part of the healthy school or SRE policy development task group.

✓ Identifying pupils' needs through surveys and interviews and collating this as part of the baseline data that informs policy and practice development.

✓ In the school council to advocate for better SRE.

✓ Meeting with governors to discuss SRE.

✓ As peer educators involved in delivering and supporting aspects of SRE.

Partnerships

A number of partnerships need to be in place in the development and delivery of PSHE and Citizenship. These include:

✓ Children and young people (see participation).

✓ Parents and carers.

✓ Wider community including religious leaders.

✓ Primary Care Trusts, Local Education Authority, School Health Nurses, Voluntary Organisations.

✓ Local Healthy Schools Programme.

✓ Local business (for example, to sponsor activities or provide work experience opportunities).

✓ Local statutory and non-statutory agencies (e.g. for provision of specialist resources, team teaching support).

✓ Local co-ordinators such as Quality Protects Co-ordinators and Teenage Pregnancy Co-ordinators.

✓ National organisations which provide support materials, advice, support and information.

Policy

A policy needs to address and include:

✓ Information about the school and the process for policy development.

✓ The aims of SRE.

✓ What will be covered including reference to statutory requirements, good practice guidance and how it relates to school, local and national priorities.

Practice - Curriculum Development

The curriculum should be developed from the policy framework. The following issues need to be considered during curriculum development:

✓ Is the curriculum relevant to children's development?

✓ Does the curriculum enable pupils to develop core skills and values including emotional resourcefulness?

✓ How it will be organised and covered. ✓ How it will meet the needs of all pupils including those who are marginalised and vulnerable. ✓ Who is responsible for co-ordinating and delivering SRE as part of PSHE and Citizenship. ✓ The values framework for SRE within the school. ✓ How pupil learning will be monitored and assessed. ✓ How it links to other policies including confidentiality and bullying. ✓ How professional development needs will be identified and met. ✓ How the policy will be monitored and reviewed and when.	✓ Are the objectives for each lesson clear and specific? ✓ Is the curriculum challenging for pupils? ✓ Are a range of teaching methods used that match the aims and objectives? ✓ Are pupils able to achieve their own level? ✓ Does the curriculum build on prior learning? How is learning reinforced? ✓ How will pupil learning be monitored, assessed and progress recorded? ✓ Will outside visitors be involved, if so, how will you ensure the quality of the input? ✓ Are resources inclusive of all pupils? ✓ Will the classroom need rearranging to ensure a safe learning environment? ✓ How does SRE relate to other curriculum priorities such as ICT and literacy? ✓ How are puipils connected to community services relevant to the curriculum? ✓ Is SRE delivered by appropriately trained staff? ✓ Are there opportunities for Personal, Social Development across the whole curriculum and how is it co-ordinated?

Figure 2.1 The four cornerstones of effective SRE

Primary and secondary schools should consult parents and pupils, both on what is included and how it should be delivered. For example, for some children it is not culturally appropriate to address particular issues in a mixed group. Consulting pupils and their families helps establish what is appropriate and acceptable for them.

Once SRE has been identified as an area for development the following steps will be helpful:

- Set up a working group.
- Audit what the school is already doing (this may involve pupil surveys).
- Identify strengths and gaps in provision and use this information to:
  - review and develop policy;
  - review and design schemes of work that fit within a broader framework of PSHE and Citizenship;
  - agree monitoring and assessment processes for SRE;
  - agree roles and responsibilities of staff, pupils and visitors;
  - identify professional development needs and plan accordingly.
- Set targets for the development of SRE taking account of issues such as:
  - national and local priorities;
  - legal requirements for SRE;
  - inequalities and inclusion.

Careful planning at this stage will ensure that SRE meets children's needs.

Set up a working group
A small group of people can be responsible for the initial development stages. This should involve:

- pupil representation, possibly from the school council;
- PSHE and Citizenship/Healthy School Co-ordinator;
- a member of the Senior Management Team;
- parent representation;
- governor representation;
- the school nurse;
- representation from the local community, e.g. relevant faith or minority ethnic community and voluntary groups.

Review existing policy and practice
Your local healthy school programme will have an audit tool to help review existing practice. (There is an example of an audit tool on pp. 120–1.) The review will need to include:

- school policies including related policies such as confidentiality;
- the whole-school ethos to consider whether the school provides a supportive ethos for SRE;

- any documentation relating to SRE. This may include Ofsted reports, previous audits or monitoring and assessment work from pupils and staff;
- training, support and resources available for SRE.

Identify pupils' needs

> We should be given a say in what we want to know. Teachers should do a little research; perhaps do a survey or something to find out what we want to know. (young woman)

Obtaining the views and opinions of children and young people on existing provision is an essential part of the process. Their views, ideas and opinions are helpful in developing governors' and parents' support for SRE. It is important to try and gain the views of different groups of pupils including boys and girls and pupils with different faiths or cultural traditions.

Information about existing provision and ideas for improving SRE can be collected through written surveys and focus groups. Older pupils could undertake surveys with young pupils as part of Citizenship. Data collected could be used in Maths to learn about collating data and representing it in graphs. School council members can survey their peers during tutorials.

It is important to try and ascertain the sexual attitudes and behaviour of pupils anonymously so that SRE can meet local needs. This can be done through anonymous surveys of pupils. Many health authorities routinely collect information about the health of young people. Data from these types of surveys can be used to influence SRE. National research such as the Ofsted report on good practice will also need to inform the development of SRE.

Identify parents', staff and community needs and views
Consultation should take place with members of the community as well as with the wide range of workers such as school nurses and Connexions Advisers who are involved in SRE. Consultation includes representatives from local religious and minority ethnic communities to ensure that the policies reflect parents' wishes and the culture of the community they serve (DfEE 2000: 7).

Consulting with parents, carers and the wider community in a structured way enables constructive dialogue. Schools that work with parents in the development of school policy and practice have found that it builds confidence in and support for school-based SRE. Consultation methods should provide opportunities to explore what is considered positive about existing practice, what causes concern or needs further development. The consultation should also provide opportunities to consider the values that will underpin SRE.

Research suggests that some parents may be anxious about attending an event that is solely about SRE. Successful strategies have included holding a general health or PSHE meeting and including information about SRE at parents' evenings.

The SRE *Guidance* emphasises the expertise and contribution that can be made by workers in the community such as those from health, formal and informal education (teaching and non-teaching staff), voluntary organisations and peer educators.

Consider local public health issues, national initiatives, legislation and policy guidance

Government guidance
- *Sex and Relationship Education Guidance* (DfEE 0116/2000)
- Personal, Social, Health Education and Citizenship Frameworks (National Curriculum Handbooks)
- National Healthy School Standard - *Guidance* and *Getting Started*

Local guidance
- Local Education Authority SRE or PSHE and Citizenship Guidance
- Local Healthy School Programme Guidance

Local data
- Use information from local profiles to ascertain trends or particular local issues. Your teenage pregnancy co-ordinator will have details of teenage pregnancy at local ward level.
- The Primary Care Trust may have carried out a survey of health needs
- School nurse health profile for schools

National Resources
- PASSPORT – a Framework for Personal, Social Development (Lees and Plant 2001)
- The Framework for Sex and Relationships Education (Sex Education Forum 1999)
- This step-by-step guide to SRE for teachers

Draft policy including values framework
This includes:

- a definition of SRE and how it fits within PSHE and Citizenship;
- a description of how SRE is provided and who is responsible for providing it;
- a section on specific issues relevant to the school community;
- a description of how it will be monitored and evaluated;
- information about parents' right to withdrawal;
- targets for the development of SRE and indicators of successful implementation;
- a monitoring and review date;
- links to other policies such as confidentiality and equal opportunities.

As with all other curriculum subjects, teachers have a professional responsibility to ensure that SRE is taught within the agreed values framework of the school and that their own values do not influence the teaching of SRE. This will ensure a school maintains the principles of equal opportunities and anti-discriminatory practice within the classroom.

The statement of values within the National Curriculum Handbooks and the school's mission statement provide a good starting point from which to consult with pupils, parents, carers and the community in order to develop an agreed values framework for SRE.

Consult on draft policy

- Who will be consulted?
- How will feedback be obtained from pupils, parents, carers and members of the community?
- Who will be responsible for obtaining feedback?
- When will it be completed?

Revise in light of comments

- Who will be responsible for this?
- When will this be completed?

Disseminate information and implement policy

- Who will receive the policy (teaching staff, non-teaching staff)?
- Who will offer support and answer any questions?
- What training and support will people need?
- What information will be offered to pupils, parents and carers?
- Who is responsible for implementation?
- When will dissemination be completed?

Monitoring the implementation and review

- How will monitoring take place, e.g. surveys of pupils or staff?
- How will feedback from pupils, parents and staff be obtained?
- Who will collate and feed back this information to the Senior Management Team?
- How will success be measured?
- When will the policy next be reviewed?

Parent's right of withdrawal

Even if effective consultation with parents takes place, there will be a very small minority of parents who choose to exercise their legal right to withdraw children from SRE. This does not mean that you are doing a bad job. Some parents will wish to educate their child about sex and relationships themselves. This should not mean that the programme is compromised significantly to avoid withdrawal.

Confidentiality policy

The SRE policy needs to be linked to a clear policy on confidentiality that will affect all aspects of school life. Teachers and others involved in SRE are often unclear about confidentiality. The advice in the Department for Education and Employment (DfEE 1994) and Welsh Office Circulars is not legally binding. The DfEE's Child Protection Circular 10/95 clarifies the position of schools regarding child protection issues.

A confidentiality policy needs to be clear, meet the best interests of pupils and be workable by all staff. It also needs to be communicated to pupils so they are clear about what they can expect. A confidentiality policy should include the following components:

- an explanation as to how pupils and parents will be made aware of the policy and how it works in practice;
- reassurance for pupils that their best interests will be maintained at all times;
- encouragement and support for pupils to talk to their parents and carers where possible;
- clarity for pupils so they know that teachers will not always be able to maintain confidentiality and if relevant who within the school can do so;
- reassurance for pupils that if confidentiality is broken, they will be told beforehand of the reason and offered support as appropriate;
- clear links to the child protection policy if abuse is disclosed;
- clear guidance for teachers about when and where they need to break confidentiality;
- a guarantee that pupils will be told where they can access support and information.

Curriculum planning and resourcing including working with external agencies

Schemes of work are developed in line with statutory requirements and best practice guidance. In addition, they reflect the local culture and issues that affect pupils. For example, in South Wales following a health survey, it was recognised that alcohol was playing a large part in their pupils' relationships and their ability to look after their sexual health. As a result, the school carried out further work on alcohol and risk taking.

School nursing profiles can provide information about local trends and issues including teenage pregnancy rates and alcohol use. Other data sets can be used including research carried out by Primary Care Trusts.

Rotherham Primary Care Trust undertook a series of consultations with young people to ascertain their needs in relation to sexual health. This information was then shared with teachers at a SRE conference.

Oxfordshire Healthy Schools Scheme is using school nurse health profiles to gain information about young people's sexual health and behaviour. This information is used to inform school audit, priorities and curriculum planning.

An integrated curriculum

Children and young people tell us that their SRE focuses on the biology and 'technical aspects', fails to help them explore 'real-life dilemmas' and develop skills such as 'being yourself in a relationship'. If we view PSHE and Citizenship in a topic-based fashion (such as sex education, drug education, mental health), the curriculum is likely to focus on information provision and ignore co-ordinated skills development and values clarification. It is unnecessary to provide pupils with vast amounts of information about sexually transmitted infections or contraception. Much more important is a focus supporting their confidence and skills to access this information either via the Internet or through a health professional.

There are core skills and values that are central to pupils' personal and social development. Curriculum time is generally tight for PSHE and Citizenship. Focusing on the development of core skills and the clarification of positive values will enable specific information about sex and sexual health to be part of a holistic programme that maximises curriculum time. For example, core skills and values include decision-making, negotiation, assertiveness and acceptance of difference. These skills and values can be explored through an activity that focuses on a topic such as sex, mental health or drugs. If a lesson is focusing on pressure in sexual relationships, links can be made to other aspects of life by asking explicit questions such as 'do you think that it might be different if we were talking about taking ecstasy, smoking or eating?' Making these explicit links avoids the need to repeat the same skills development with a number of different topics.

Using 'real-life' scenarios supports an integrated curriculum and addresses a wide range of issues for children and young people and can explore information needs, skills development and values clarification. At the primary level a scenario about teasing a girl whose body is changing will bring up factual information about puberty and different pubertal development, skills development such as asking for help, being assertive and values clarification such as the unacceptability of bullying and acceptance of diversity and difference. These skills and values will be relevant across many areas of children's lives and explicit links can be made through effective questioning.

At the secondary level a scenario about going to a party could bring up all sorts of issues for young people including alcohol and drug use, safety, peer pressure, and body image as well as providing opportunities to develop skills and try out responses to different situations.

Where in the curriculum: planning

Guidance from the Qualifications and Curriculum Authority on PSHE and Citizenship (QCA 2000) suggests that when planning, schools should include opportunities in three curriculum locations:

- *Designated curriculum time.* Where there is sufficient support for a specialist team of teachers, designated courses have status with pupils who enjoy and benefit from structured and safe learning opportunities.

21

- *Teaching PSHE and Citizenship in and through other subject/curriculum areas.* Some subjects such as Science, Religious Education and English can provide a focus for discussing some elements of SRE.
- *Occasional off-timetable experiences, such as 'health days'* provide a useful focus for an intensive study of SRE and encourage active citizenship. They should form part of a carefully planned ongoing SRE curriculum. Many schools work together with other schools in their area to develop these types of events. One cluster of secondary schools, led by a working group of pupils, brought together all the community advisory and support services in the area. Pupils were offered workshops by different services to identify and clarify what they offered, when and how. These events offer positive opportunities for pupils to learn planning and organisation skills as well as building confidence in accessing community services.

As with all lesson planning it is important that clear aims and objectives are set for each lesson as well as the series of lessons. Activities have clear educational outcomes that are possible to monitor. There will need to be a broad aim for the whole of the programme such as 'to support pupils' confidence in their interpersonal relationships'.

To meet that aim, lesson planning must help pupils to:

- learn to communicate assertively by developing listening skills, expressing their opinions and resolving conflict;
- gain information about sex, sexuality, sexual health and relationships including information about contraception, sexually transmitted infections and HIV ;
- consider how their own morals and values affect their attitudes and behaviour regarding sex and relationships.

When planning activities that meet these objectives a number of issues need to be considered:

- What are you trying to achieve?
- What activity will best secure the outcome?
- How big is the group?
- Is the room suitable?
- How well do the group know each other?
- Does the group feel safe?
- How well do you know the group?
- Will it meet the needs of all pupils within the group e.g. boys, girls, gay pupils, pupils from black and minority ethnic communities?
- Are all members of the group able to do the same task?
- What do the group know already?
- Do you have any classroom support?
- Do you have the confidence and experience to run a specific activity?

Linking with other curriculum areas enhances the opportunities for learning about sex and relationships. Other subjects can complement SRE:

- English – Fiction often addresses relationships issues. Relevant books can be offered as part of the English curriculum, and in particular books can be chosen as part of the school literacy improvement strategy. An article, 'Read all about it!', exploring the use of children's literature is available on the Sex Education Forum website www.ncb.org.uk/sexed.htm
- Maths and Information Communication Technology – Pupils can collect data about their peers' satisfaction with SRE, or levels of knowledge about local services, and develop graphs and charts to present the data. They then use ICT to present this data.

  Pupils also research information on the Internet. This might include searching for websites where children and young people can access help and support or gathering statistics.
- Religious Education provides opportunities for discussion of issues relating to sex and relationships.

> The Hardley School in Hampshire was commended by Ofsted (2002) for their work in Religious Education on relationships. The pupils were considering relationships in society. Pupils discussed why young people might or might not have a sexual relationship. Using different methods, pupils were encouraged to think about acting within an agreed moral framework.

- Citizenship provides opportunities for exploring sex and relationships issues. For example, pupils could take undertake research about services in their community. In Birmingham a group of young people went along to sexual health services across the city and critiqued them. All the information was then drawn together and fed back to service providers with their ideas for improving them.

  Pupils can undertake projects focusing on the global impact of HIV, or different perspectives on sexuality and abortion. Pupils can also practise listening to and expressing different opinions about a range of different social and moral issues.
- Media Studies – pupils undertake a critical analysis of the messages presented in the media about teenage sex, homosexuality and gender.
- Assemblies provide a focus for one-off events. Many schools carry out interactive assemblies led by pupils as part of World AIDS Day campaigns.

Choosing and using resources

Resources help in the planning and delivery of sex and relationships education. No resource, however, will be able to be used in its entirety and most will need some adaptation in order to meet the needs of your particular pupils. Resources can be used to trigger discussion and thinking within the classroom.

There are a range of resources that are available to help you in the delivery of sex and relationships education. Whether the resource is purchased or offered free, you need to be sure that it is going to meet the needs of all your pupils.

The SRE *Guidance* from the DfEE emphasises the importance of choosing and using appropriate resources. The checklist below will help you in deciding which resources to use:

- Is it consistent with the school ethos, mission statement, equal opportunities statement and the values framework for SRE?
- Is it appropriate to the needs of your pupils in terms of language, images, attitude, maturity and understanding and the knowledge required?
- Does it avoid racism, sexism, gender and homophobic stereotyping? Does it exclude anyone on the basis of home circumstance, gender, race, literacy, culture, disability, faith or religion?
- Does it include positive images of a range of children and young people?
- Can it be used as trigger material for discussions of difference or exclusiveness?
- Can the resource be adapted for use with particular groups of children and young people?
- Is it factually correct and up to date?
- Video resources – are these current enough in terms of fashion, are there images of different children and young people? Will the pupils be able to relate to the visual images, e.g. fashion, etc.?
- Will the resource contribute to a broad and balanced PSHE and Citizenship curriculum?
- Does it encourage active and participatory learning methods?
- If you have used this resource before, what formal or informal feedback did you receive from children and young people about it?
- Are you confident about using the resource?

Using videos
There are many sex and relationships education videos. Many of them are very good but they can date quickly in terms of image and fashion. The accent or ethnicity of the actors can also influence how pupils engage with a video. This does not necessarily mean that they cannot be used, but ask yourself, how will you address this with the pupils? One strategy is to explicitly talk about the different accent or say that it was made a few years ago and then ask them to think about whether things are different in another part of the country or whether things have changed over time. Often the pupils are surprised at how similar the issues are and it can in fact be a really positive entry point. Most videos are too long to be viewed in one go. It is important that time is allowed for discussion about the issues raised in the video.

Some young people reviewed a series of SRE videos at the Sex Education Forum and one of the key criticisms was that they seemed to be what adults believe young people think will be interesting and informative.

Videoing a short clip from a television programme such as *EastEnders* or watching a film such as *Billy Elliot* can be just as effective in stimulating discussions and ideas.

Northumberland Sex Education Forum has a working group who review resources and then recommend resources for use within schools. This supports teachers' confidence in using resources.

Partnerships

Partnerships really help move things forward. Recognition of the need for health and education to work together is evident through the government funding of the National Healthy School Standard. Alliances can be school-based and involve teaching and non-teaching staff including Connexions Advisers and the school nurse working together to plan and deliver SRE. They can be locality based. Multi-agency partnerships enable workers to share and learn from each other and to maximise their different skills.

Working in partnership across education, health and the voluntary sector has positive benefits for all concerned including:

- a consistency of approach with a shared values framework;
- sharing skills and expertise and contributing to professional development;
- maximising human and financial resources;
- providing links between the school and community services;
- providing opportunities for visitors in the classroom which can enrich the curriculum;
- promoting inter-agency work;
- the development of joint educational and health objectives that can contribute to school improvement aims and public health priorities such as teenage pregnancy and sexual health. For example, locally within education there may be a concern with boys' under-achievement and within health a focus on working with boys as part of efforts to reduce teenage pregnancy. An activity to meet both of these strategic objectives might include the exploration of masculinity and gender issues within PSHE and Citizenship.

To be effective, partnerships need to:

- be clear about the needs that have to be met;
- be clear about the resources and expertise available locally;
- be clear about the roles and responsibilities of individuals;
- have clear and shared objectives that can be monitored and present clear indicators of success.

Key partners who can support schools in developing policy and practice are:

- local Healthy Schools Programme including LEA Advisory Support;
- outside visitors and external agencies;
- youth workers;
- school nurses;
- voluntary agencies.

Local Healthy Schools Programme

All local programmes are accredited to the National Standard and therefore have the capacity and capability to support schools to improve SRE. Local programmes will offer different types of support but all will help provide a framework for auditing existing practice and development planning. LEA Advisory staff are a key partner in local programmes. Most LEAs offer an open training course programme, INSET and consultancy generally as a part of the Healthy Schools Programme.

Outside visitors and external agencies

Outside visitors and external agencies can enhance a SRE programme. When inviting outside visitors it is important that they know and understand the policy and values framework of the school and work within it. Careful planning is necessary to ensure that the visitor and the school are aware of the role and responsibilities of each party as well as how the session will fit into the broader SRE curriculum. Where individuals are working within schools it is important they work within the schools' SRE policy. Teachers need to be confident that the visitor will provide a broad and balanced perspective and that they are working to clear learning objectives. This will require planning so that:

- learning objectives are clear;
- preparation can be done. This may involve the pupils writing down the questions that they have before the visit;
- the classroom is laid out properly so that 'contact time' is not wasted in preparing the room;
- equipment is agreed; and
- follow-up work is agreed.

There are some organisations with a particular moral and values framework that offer services to schools. Their aim is to shock and frighten pupils. A polemic approach is not conducive to effective learning and is disrespectful of diversity. Some of these organisations will provide incorrect information. This is particularly true on issues relating to sexuality and abortion and is clearly not acceptable.

> Somerset Healthy Schools Programme has developed a booklet on working with external agencies. It provides a checklist of issues that each party should consider and provides a clear planning framework including the roles and responsibilities of both parties.

Youth workers

Trained youth workers are generally competent in using active learning methods and developing issue-based work in informal settings. They offer expertise and support through team teaching in the classroom, supporting visits to local sexual health services and providing lunchtime or after school sessions targeting marginalised, vulnerable or friendship groups.

School nurses

Confident and trained school nurses are an obvious source of information and support for schools. The school nurse role should support that of the teachers. When they are working in a classroom which is a public place, they work within the SRE policy, including the policy on confidentiality – irrespective of whom they are employed by. This is because they are acting as an educator. When they are acting as a nurse in private consultations, they work within their own professional guidelines.

School nurses are in an ideal position to team-teach with teachers to support them in developing skills, knowledge and confidence in SRE. This type of co-facilitation has proved helpful for using active learning methods.

The Department of Health are currently exploring an accreditation process for school nurses who teach SRE. For further information see the Forum Factsheet: 'The Role of the School Nurse in Sex and Relationships Education', available on the SEF website: www.ncb.org.uk/sexed.htm.

Voluntary agencies

There are many sexual health and HIV voluntary agencies who are willing to go into schools and support SRE. Some will charge a fee, others will ask for a donation and some will be free.

Brook London Education Outreach Team works in schools as part of a multi-agency approach. They offer help in developing programmes for the whole school, supporting INSET training and professional development opportunities for teachers and representation on appropriate forums.

The worker follows a checklist to ensure that schools are clear about their needs and how the intervention will fit in with a programme, including how the work will be evaluated.

They also contribute to multi-agency drop-in sessions that are run in the schools to provide information and referral advice to a range of services.

Talk About Choice is a project run by Education For Choice. Workers visit schools to facilitate discussion on unplanned pregnancy and abortion. For a talk with a large group the emphasis is on disseminating information with plenty of time for questions and answers. In a group of 30, workers use the factual information as a basis for a more in-depth discussion of abortion as a social issue, how to access appropriate advice and services to prevent, or cope with, an unplanned pregnancy and to explore – through the use of continuums, quizzes and structured discussion – the attitudes and values that will shape their decisions.

For further information contact Education for Choice (see Useful organisations list, p. 126).

In many areas of the country there are local Sex Education Forums or local practice development networks. These are multi-agency groups where teachers, youth workers, school nurses and other workers can come together to share ideas and develop good practice.

The networks are organised differently. Some are organised by health authorities, some through education and others through local healthy school programmes.

> Sheffield Sexual Health Forum offers meetings which provide a short speaker input on a theme or piece of local practice and opportunities to view resources and small group work. These meetings are always well evaluated and are perceived to be a positive and relatively economical approach to supporting professional development and networking in local areas.

The Sex Education Forum factsheet, 'Setting up a Local Network', is available at www.ncb.org.uk/sef

There are a number of different websites that can support curriculum planning:

- Wired for Health www.wiredforhealth.co.uk
- National Grid for Learning www.ngfl.gov.uk
- Local healthy schools website – contact your local healthy schools programme for details
- DfES PSHE and Citizenship websites www.teachernet.gov.uk/pshe; www.dfes.gov.uk/citizenship/
- Sex Education Forum website www.ncb.org.uk/sef

3 Developing and delivering SRE

SRE is delivered using a range of methods. Research with young people shows that they are unhappy with SRE that uses traditional didactic methods (Thomson and Scott 1991). When asked, a group of year 5 children said: 'It needs to be fun, you need to be able to have a go.' Young people often feel that they are 'talked to' in SRE. They want to discuss different ideas and learn from each other (Sex Education Forum 2000). *'It would be helpful to have more role-plays, more practical things and less worksheets. Involve pupils and have debates and discussions' (young woman aged 14).*

Ofsted (2002) identified the following features of good teaching:

- Teachers have a broad and detailed understanding of the aspects of SRE they teach.
- A clear focus for lesson planning.
- Expectations of the pupils that are appropriate to their differing levels of maturity and understanding.
- Creating a climate that encourages pupils to express their views and feelings and to respect the views of others with clearly established boundaries for both courtesy and confidentiality.
- Teaching methods, including good use of resources, give good opportunities for pupils to reflect on and assimilate learning.
- Assessment of pupils' knowledge and understanding and, in the best practice, of the development of their attitudes and values and their personal skills.

Research into the effectiveness of SRE has shown that active learning methods are central to success (Kirby 1997). Ofsted's report (2002) on SRE identifies the importance of active learning methodologies. Using these methods will contribute to a pupil's personal, social development and their ability to learn effectively. The elements of effective SRE are:

- knowledge;
- skills;
- emotions;
- attitudes and values.

These are shown in Figure 3.1.

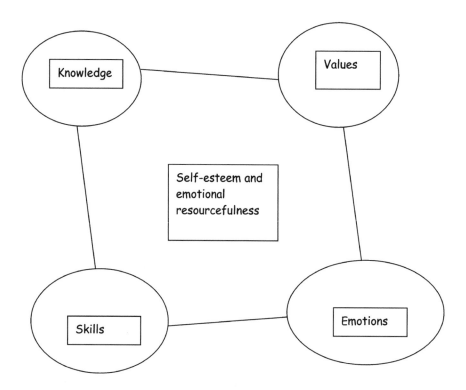

Figure 3.1 The elements of effective sex and relationships education

Active learning methods enable these four elements to be included and will enable children and young people to develop self-esteem and emotional resourcefulness as well as a positive attitude to sex and sexual health and relevant skills.

So, for example, the relevant elements of learning about sexually transmitted infections (STIs) include:

- Information about the range of STIs, how they are contracted and how they are prevented.
- Skills, including negotiation skills for safer sex, saying no and accessing sexual health help and advice.
- Positive values clarification includes exploration of stereotypes about the 'type' of person who contracts STIs, the importance of safer sex and an acceptance of diversity.
- Emotions elements include what it might feel like to get help, advice and support or to negotiate safer sex.

Covering these four different elements supports the development of self-esteem, a sense of identity and confidence in managing relationships.

What is active learning?

Active learning works by using creative processes to develop skills. Active learning works primarily within a group setting where children and young people work together **as** a group. The group is then used to learn from each other and practise using the knowledge and skills within that group. The experience of listening to others' views and beliefs, practising skills, observing others and developing relationships supports learning.

The principle behind active learning lies in a sequence of different parts of the learning process which diagrammatically is represented in Figure 3.2.

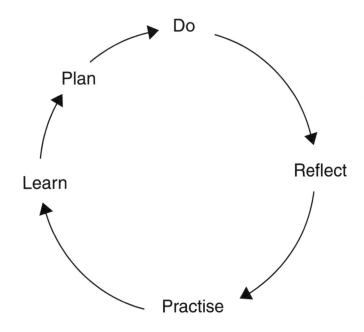

Figure 3.2 Elements of active learning

The processes involved in active learning

Doing – taking part in a structured activity, finding out information, exploring beliefs and values or practising skills. For example, pupils could undertake a decision-making exercise where they are asked to decide on a course of action that a young person might take, based on a case study such as: Rosie and Paul have been going out together for about four months. Rosie wants to have sex with Paul. Paul does not feel ready. Rosie is angry with Paul and keeps asking him what is wrong with him. She is worried that maybe he does not fancy her.

The case study might have a series of questions such as:

- What might Paul be feeling?
- What might Paul be thinking?
- What might Paul do?
- What might be the consequences?
- What might Rosie be feeling?
- What might Rosie be thinking?
- What might Rosie do?
- What might be the consequences?

This activity can be done in small groups. Each group works together to think about the answers to the questions. They then come together to reflect upon the activity and discuss their ideas: 'We think that Paul should decide not to have sex with Rosie if he does not feel ready.'

Reflecting – pupils are helped to reflect on the process through the use of open questions. For example:

Teacher: What made you think that this was the right decision?

Pupils: We thought about the choices that are available and thought that the most important thing was that he did not do anything he did not want to.

Practising – by critically working out what happened, for example:

Teacher: So when you looked at the choices that were available to him, how did you work out that what Paul wanted to do was the most important? Did you think about the other options available to him?

Pupil: Even though it might be difficult because he thinks his girlfriend might dump him, we thought that if she does not respect him, then it would not be a very good relationship anyway.

Teacher: How could Paul talk about this to Rosie?

Pupil: He should tell her how he feels and make sure she knows it is because he does not feel ready to have sex yet and make sure she knows it is not because he does not fancy her.

Learning from the activity and applying the learning – at this stage the young people are encouraged to think about what has been learnt and how they might use this learning, for example:

Teacher: So if somebody was in either Rosie or Paul's situation in the future, what might they do?

Pupil: Make sure that they talk to the other person and explain why they feel or think what they do. Really try to make sure they understand each other and talk about it.

Good SRE resources provide activities that are based on active learning principles. A number of techniques and ideas are outlined on pp. 40–2, 84–7.

What are the benefits of using active learning methods?

Active learning methods have a number of benefits:

- Children and young people are acknowledged as the starting point for their own learning and can draw on their own experiences to aid learning and understanding.
- Children and young people undertake the task at the level they are able to, hence meeting the different abilities of people within the group (see Differentiated learning on p. 39).
- Children and young people experience a positive and respectful relationship with the teachers and other pupils.
- Children, young people and staff find them interesting and fun.
- Using different learning methods increases the interest and energy of the children, young people and teachers.
- Children and young people respond to the content and understand the broad range of beliefs, opinions, feelings, views and ideas of the other people in the group.
- Children and young people have the opportunity to develop and practise critical analysis or self-reflection, to make decisions and find consensus or agree to differ.
- The process of working as a group enables the development of personal and social skills such as working in teams, listening, or speaking in groups. These skills are core education skills and support the development of children and young people as lifelong learners and active citizens.

Practical skills

- for everyday living such as decision-making;
- for supporting others such as listening skills;
- for relationships generally and future parenting through the development of skills such as empathy and understanding;
- use of Information Technology.

Communication skills

- listening to the views of others and being able to put forward their own views and ideas without trying to change the views of others;
- giving and receiving feedback including compliments;
- handling conflict assertively and confidently and being able to agree to differ or work to develop a consensus view.

Decision-making skills

- the ability to make safe and healthy judgements and decisions based on the information available;
- the ability to say no or yes based on their own views and not feel forced by others;
- making moral judgements about situations and developing the skills to act on these judgements;
- acting responsibly as an individual and as a member of various groups including family, class group, school community, etc.

Inter-personal skills

- for managing relationships confidently;
- for being an active member of a group;
- to play their part as an active citizen within the community.

Problem-solving skills

- that support independent thought and critical thinking;
- developing their own moral and values framework.

Leadership and team work skills

- for taking different roles in groups;
- for taking the initiative;
- for supporting and managing others;
- of compromise.

How groups work

All groups go through a particular process of development. Methods of teaching and content need to match the stage in a group's development. There are different models of group process but all describe a similar process (Schutz 1965; Tuckman 1965). The following is based on Tuckman's work.

Forming – the starting process when pupils are likely to feel shy, excited or unsure especially if there is something new happening or if this is a new way of working. Some may find both the process and the content worrying.

Teachers support the group through this stage. This can be done by ensuring that everyone gets an opportunity to contribute, through the negotiation of clear working agreements, and giving clear instructions about what they are expected to do.

Storming – pupils may feel insecure and may argue about what they are doing and how they are going to do it. They may have difficulties in understanding instructions.

Again, confidence is important at this stage in the group development, as is giving plenty of encouragement and support for the group. Teachers build the confidence of the group and therefore tasks that are relevant and not too challenging are helpful. If they do not understand the instructions, try repeating them in a different way.

Norming – as the confidence of the group grows, they begin to settle down and work out who is going to do what. They are now more interested in the task and together working through their own personal anxieties and concerns.

The teacher now begins to rely on the pupils to get on with the task. The teacher's role is primarily about support and clarification. Some individuals may still need extra support to integrate into the group fully.

Performing – having worked out how they are going to work together and what they want to achieve, pupils do their best work together. They will have understood what is expected of them and trust both the teacher and the group.

The teacher's role here is to allow the group to carry out the task and be available for help and support if they request it.

Building the group

To enable the group to work well together, time will need to be spent building the group trust and cohesion. If they are worried about what they are going to do, or how it is going to be done, they will concentrate on that and not on the task, so the time will be well spent, as it will enable the pupils to get to the *performing* stage and hence maximise the learning.

When working in any group attention needs to be paid to the individual, the group and the task. An over-emphasis on the task can prevent the learning from being effective. Paying attention to these three elements will help to prevent the group from going off track. Throughout the process the teacher needs to ask:

- How is the group working?
- Is everyone engaged?
- Is the task getting completed?

If the group begin to stop working the teacher should ask:

- Is the task too easy or too hard?
- Is one individual dominating?
- Are the group helping one another?
- Do individuals need something, e.g. a break, the task clarifying or an opportunity to express concerns about the content or style?

Teaching methods for SRE

The following process and skills have all proved to be effective in developing a safe learning environment in which children and young people can feel confident exploring and learning about sex and relationships.

Working agreements – The National Healthy School Standard *Guidance* (1999a) emphasises the importance of creating a safe environment. Working agreements are often called ground rules. The use of the term agreements signifies a shift in power and offers an agreement that everyone agrees to. Negotiating these with the class provides an opportunity to consider the boundaries within the classroom. It also provides a positive message that this is going to be an environment where people are going to behave respectfully with one another. This then reduces anxiety and embarrassment. It also reduces the risk of unintended personal 'disclosure'.

Confidentiality is not a realistic agreement. The classroom is a public place and pupils need to know that they cannot and should not expect confidentiality in the classroom but should be aware of other sources of confidential advice and support such as the school nurse/school councillor and sexual health services in the community.

The following is an example from King Edward VII School in Sheffield:

> Be friendly.
> Be nice.
> Listen to each other.
> Try to understand each other.
> Get along and treat each other with respect.
> Help each other out.
> Share your feelings.
> Get to know each other well.
> Be supportive of each other.
> Show you care.
> Do not hurt each other.
> Do not make fun of each other.
> Don't treat me like I'm different.

Language is negotiated at this stage so that everyone understands and is comfortable with the language used.

Offer clear boundaries – at the beginning of the session clarify what is going to happen and what people are going to do. Explaining what you are trying to achieve allows the pupils to recognise when they have achieved the objective of the session.

Do not offer personal experience – although it may be tempting, it can cause pupils to think that they are expected to do the same. This can make the group feel unsafe and could lead to bullying if pupils were to disclose information.

Participation of pupils in the planning, delivery and monitoring of SRE ensures that it is relevant to their needs. For example, if inviting outside visitors to support the programme, pupils could write a letter explaining the type of issues that they would like addressed within the session.

Setting the agenda with pupils so that they have an opportunity to contribute to the learning objectives helps ensure relevance and interest. One of the key things that pupils say is 'They told us what they think we should know' and 'It was really good when you asked us what we wanted to learn'.

The following is a list of issues that Year 7 pupils at the King Edward VII School in Sheffield wanted to discuss.

> We would like to discuss . . .
>
> drugs   friendship   feelings   bullying   people   safety
>
> peer pressure   sex education   racism   problems
>
> health education   smoking   social skills   anger management
>
> divorce   the family   relationships
>
> parents who separate and meet other people

Sometimes it might appear that what pupils want is different from your agenda. Through clarification the issues are generally similar; for example, a group of young men wanted to talk about 'chat up lines'. After discussion and clarification their concerns included: 'how you go and talk to someone sensibly', 'how it feels if you get rejected' and 'the embarrassment of talking to somebody you do not know'. This demonstrates how the starting points for discussion may be different but, through clarification, many of the core issues within SRE can be addressed and explored.

Developing rituals enables pupils to feel confident and comfortable and creates a safe environment. By following a similar process for each lesson pupils feel confident in the process and therefore engage more fully with the content. So, for example, always starting with a reminder of the working agreement, an icebreaker followed by a recap on previous learning before the main task enables pupils to feel confident with the process.

Task setting – set clear and specific tasks. Pupils often report that SRE did not feel like work and it was not concrete enough. Rather than setting a general task such as 'discuss this scenario', ask very specific questions that provide a positive focus. Questions for a scenario might include:

- What do you think might influence the decisions?
- Whom do you think they might be able to talk to about their choices?
- What might be the consequences of their actions?

Offer a time frame for the exercise and be specific about the feedback that is required. For example, 'You will be asked to report back three things that might influence their decision and to identify who you think is the most likely person they could talk to about their choices.'

Be confident in the activity that you are asking them to undertake. Sometimes pupils can be hesitant to begin an activity or exercise if they feel your anxiety. Be firm and confident.

Repetition and reinforcement are essential to connect learning. Pupils need time to assimilate learning and develop skills. As with all subject areas, aspects of SRE should be revisited. Repetition is particularly important for pupils with learning disabilities who may require greater opportunities to reinforce the learning. At the beginning of a lesson asking pupils to talk to a partner and discuss three things that were covered in the last session is a positive way to reinforce learning. Helping pupils to record learning in log books or a folder provides opportunities for reflection and reinforcement.

Provide encouragement and offer positive feedback – reward pupils who participate effectively within the group. It has been suggested that human beings need ten positive comments to one criticism to flourish and grow (Kline 1998). Offer positive feedback as a model. Pupils, boys in particular, often say that adults are very quick to point out when they do something wrong, but less quick to praise them when they have behaved or achieved well.

Challenge constructively – it is your responsibility to maintain a positive learning environment. Challenge that is presented inappropriately or aggressively can impede learning by alienating individuals and making them feel defensive. Refer the group back to the working agreement. Challenge can be offered implicitly, for example, by naming prejudice or using inclusive language. It can also be done gently, for example, by saying, 'I think that it is OK not to have sex'. Ask the group a question to think about, such as 'Why do you think some people think that?'

It may not always be appropriate to address an issue immediately. You could make a statement such as 'I don't believe that is true' and then revisit that later with the pupil. It is never a good idea to polarise groups by taking a strong position. It is better to refer back to the group agreement or the school's values by saying, 'That is not an acceptable thing to say in this school' and then move on.

Use a developmental approach that begins with topics that are safer, and explores attitudes and values once trust and cohesion have been established.

Use distancing techniques to encourage objectivity and support confidentiality. They allow pupils to gain information, develop skills and explore their attitudes without being personal. Use role play and case study material of children or young people like them. This will support safety by ensuring that pupils can access the information and develop skills that they need without having to say publicly that they need it. It is important that they can relate to the material. *'They were really ridiculous things, the case studies were not real' (young woman, aged 15).*

Be inclusive and affirm diversity throughout the whole of SRE. Use language such as partner instead of boyfriend and girlfriend. Talk about vaginal sex, oral sex and anal sex rather than foreplay and sex. Do not make assumptions about pupils from a particular ethnic, cultural or religious background, rather, encourage exploration.

Summarise the learning at regular intervals to help keep pupils focused on the task and to reinforce the learning and diversity of opinion. For example, say, 'This topic seems to have interested you all and there has been quite a lively discussion. Some of you think that having sex before marriage is acceptable and some of you think that it is better to wait until you are married. All of you appear to think that it is important to trust a partner before you have sex with them.'

Give opportunities for reflection by using open-ended questions to encourage pupils to think about their learning. Focus on why and how things happen rather than what happened.

Use open questions that enable discussion rather than one-word answers. An example of a closed question might be, 'Do you think that young men can access sexual health services?', whereas an open question might be, 'What do you think it might be like for a young man to access a sexual health service?'

Be available for questioning after the session. Not all pupils will feel confident to ask a question in front of the class yet may want to get further information. 'Hanging around' for five minutes to allow pupils to seek help individually is helpful.

Connect with confidential services – you will not be able to provide pupils with all the information they need and sex education lessons may encourage young people to seek further help and support (Buston and Wight 2002). Ensure that they are aware where their local services are based and what these services are able to offer by placing information on bulletin boards and distributing leaflets and credit card-type information. This should be available by contacting your local Teenage Pregnancy Co-ordinator based in the Primary Care Trust. Some schools run mock clinics (see pp. 79–80), others invite service providers into schools (see p. 80).

Differentiated learning

Pupils in any one group will have different abilities, based on their emotional and physical development, experiences, literacy levels, first language, culture and learning disabilities. Differentiated learning can be in terms of

- *Outcome* – a task for all that the group can achieve at their own level.
- *Extension of activity* – groups who finish first can be given an extra activity to further develop their understanding.
- *Support on the task* – an extra member of staff can work with a group to offer extra support. With increased learning support staff within the classroom this option is quite often available within the school's resources. This can also be achieved through the use of outside speakers.
- *Different activities* – active learning techniques allow the teacher to manage more than one activity at a time.
- *Grouping by ability* – this may be by same or mixed ability

In some circumstances it might be helpful to provide different tasks to pupils within the same group. Active learning methods allow for this flexibility.

- *Grouping by gender* – active learning techniques can allow small groups to do different tasks. For example, boys could do a task about being a boy while the girls do a task about being a girl. They could then come back and discuss their learning. Evidence suggests that both girls and boys would like to have some time in single sex groupings (Frosh *et al*. 2001; Ray 2000). Setting different tasks for boys and girls is one way of enabling this to happen within 'normal' curriculum arrangements.
- *Grouping by age* – some primary schools, particularly in rural areas, have classes of mixed age groups. Active learning methods allow the pupils to do different tasks relevant to their age group.

Some active learning methods

The following are examples of active learning methods. You will need to match the method to the purpose of the lesson and to the pupils you are working with.

Word storming is a useful way of recording ideas quickly. It helps gauge pupils' prior knowledge and identifies the range of prevailing attitudes and current concerns and issues. It should only take a few minutes. Ask pupils to call out all the words they associate with a particular word such as 'relationships'. All responses are written up, none are filtered by the teacher. The word-storm could be discussed or built on in another exercise.

Discussion techniques – asking pupils to work in small groups makes talking easier for them. For many people talking in front of a large group is very frightening and they can develop confidence working first in pairs and then in threes, etc. In order to involve *all* members of a group rather than just the confident or vocal members, it will be necessary to divide the class into various sub-groups. The following are some ideas for discussion sessions:

- Twos to fours – pupils can be asked to talk in pairs and then move into fours to share what they have learned.
- Reporting back – after a discussion/task, each group can share what they have done/talked about. This ensures that they *have done* something and shows valuing of contributions.
- Socratic discussion – this form of discussion is teacher-led with pupils working in threes being given a question to discuss for a short period (one minute) then sharing in the whole group, before leading with another question which has arisen from the discussion.
- Fishbowl discussion – this is a way of controlling discussion. Put not more than six or seven chairs in an inner circle, with the rest in an outer circle. Discussion takes place only in the inner circle. A spare chair ensures that someone can come into the centre. At the same time people in the centre can move out and allow others to contribute.
- Debates must be well prepared to be effective. Reticent pupils are more likely to take part if small group discussion has taken place prior to the formal debate. Debate can sometimes be unhelpful as opinions become polarised and pupils are forced to 'take up' a position rather than explore the complexity of issues. It may not therefore be useful for discussing issues such as abortion and homosexuality.
- Standpoint-taking – this technique enables pupils to explore both sides of an issue. Make two concentric circles with chairs, each inside chair facing an outside chair. Give a statement and ask the inside group to argue for it, and the outside group to argue against with the person they are sitting opposite. It is important to stress that they may not agree with that particular stance, but they have to find as many arguments as possible. Allow two minutes' discussion and move people in the outer circle on two places. Repeat the process. Move again but this time change stances, thus arguing the opposite viewpoint. Debrief: How did it feel to argue for something with which you disagreed? How easy was it to change viewpoints? What have you learned?
- Listening exercises – these can be conducted in pairs. For example, person A talks to person B for two or three minutes describing the qualities of a friend. Person B records for A. They swap roles. This pair joins another pair and they are asked to draw up a friend specification. This work is presented to other groups or the whole class. Friend specifications could be displayed or form part of pupil folders.
- Questionnaires and quizzes are not tests of knowledge but triggers for discussion, where pupils will be able to acquire more information as well as explore issues arising. They should not last too long otherwise some pupils may feel excluded or bored. They can be used for discussion by asking the group to mark on the questions the things they agree with or disagree with on their own and then discuss with a partner those on which they disagreed.

Myths and folklore can be used as a way of distancing learning. Ask children and young people to think about the types of myths or stories they have heard about relationships, masturbation, sex, pregnancy and infection. Pupils and teachers can then work together to clarify truths.

Trigger drawings, storyboards, situation cards, photographs, and magazine articles can be used for discussion, problem-solving or as material for role play.

Case studies can be used to help pupils to understand another person's experience and to consider the effects of the situation. It also helps them to think about a situation that they may be involved in without disclosing any personal information. The group is asked, for instance, to work out all the options that are available to the characters described – who would help them and how could they get this help?

Using visitors is a powerful group-building activity and provides pupils with the opportunity to find out what they want to know. This is an alternative to 'speakers' and gives responsibility to the group for the process and for their own learning. Pupils control the session, and visitors should be briefed that they will not be giving a presentation but will be asked to respond to questions about their area of expertise or experience. In preparing for the visit the group considers questions such as, who do we invite and for what purpose? What do we want to know? What questions shall we ask and in what order? How is everybody going to be involved? How do we make the visitor comfortable? Who will draw the session to a close? The visit should be followed by a debriefing session to draw out the learning of the subject matter and the performance of the group.

Story telling – make use of fiction to explore feelings and attitudes. Relating the discussion to the fictional characters provides a safer way of examining experiences the children/young people may go through such as making and losing friends, puberty, bullying, needing help, bereavement and many others. Refer to current situations in 'soaps'. How would the group resolve the issues raised within these stories?

Videos and films can be thought-provoking and interesting, but equally can be boring, inaccurate and outdated. It may be tempting for teachers and the audience to react passively to them. Issues raised in the video/film need to be followed up by other methods. To ensure that the video/film has educational rather than entertainment value, ask the group to look for four or five key points. These can form the basis for a group discussion. Pausing or stopping the video at key points is another way of picking up issues for discussion. The Health Education Authority states that the use of actors in dramatised situations can bring about changes in attitudes or behaviour but is most likely to do so when there are opportunities for rehearsing the situation and discussing the results afterwards (Health Education Authority 1996).

Continuums – these are 'lines' of variance between two points, such as agree or disagree, or high risk, low risk. Pupils (volunteers) are asked to physically place themselves somewhere along the line that best describes their opinion or value to a statement called out by the teacher. Care should always be taken to ensure that statements used are sensitive to the circumstances and backgrounds of the pupils. Opinions are shared with one or two others and finally opened up to the group where appropriate. After a few minutes pupils find someone of the opposite opinion and exchange views. The aim of the exercise is not to change other people's views, but to listen to and understand them. Pupils enjoy an activity that makes them move about, demonstrates the breadth of opinion so visually and offers a real opportunity to both express their values and listen to the values of others. Although this exercise can be fun and a really useful experience it must be carefully facilitated so that pupils do not feel alienated and frightened. Always affirm a pupil who finds themselves alone on the continuum, they may be teased about this afterwards.

A variation is to get children to place pictures taken from magazines along a continuum. For example:

what men do . . .	what both men and women do . . .	what women do . . .

Encourage pupils to discuss gender roles and stereotypes.

Role-play – pupils are asked to identify with a character and `act' out his/her role in a particular situation. This gives them an opportunity to experience an issue or situation from a different perspective. For instance, a girl can experience how a boy feels about asking a girl out. If pupils are to identify with their characters, careful preparation is needed to build the background and feelings of the characters before the role play takes place. Role play is sometimes used so badly that people are afraid of it. Always use role play in small groups and never ask pupils to perform in front of the class. Sometimes pupils identify strongly with their 'character' and cannot disengage, so make sure you 'de-role' the pupils. Re-engage them with the present by asking a simple question such as, 'What did you have for lunch today?'

This is just a small selection of activities. Many resources are now available that offer curriculum materials. Choose and adapt activities that will meet the needs of the pupils and suit your own personal style and the ethos of the school.

School culture, ethos and environment

SRE contributes to the school's overall aim of supporting pupils' spiritual, moral, social and cultural development. Staff, governors, parents, pupils and the wider community all need to work together to develop a positive school ethos and environment.

For children and young people to learn effectively, they need to feel safe. Repeatedly, when asked, they quote safety as being of primary importance (Forum on Children and Violence 2001). Both nationally and locally colleagues involved in the National Healthy School Standard have asked children and young people what makes a healthy school. Common responses include:

- Where there is no bullying.
- Where you can ask for help.
- Where you can ask any questions that you want to.
- Where teachers talk to you respectfully.

Often when addressing SRE, the focus is on the teaching and learning within the classroom during lessons that are explicitly called SRE. However, children and young people will learn about relationships from the school ethos and culture and from the way adults and their peers treat them.

A healthy school provides an environment in which children and young people feel safe, are safe and can do 'their best'. Healthy schools work with pupils, parents and staff as well as other members of the school community to develop activities that will support the raising of education standards and improvements in health. This is done both within the formal curriculum and in the general ethos and climate of the school.

The environment also needs to enable children and young people to move through puberty and adolescence with dignity. Bullying, including sexual and homophobic bullying, must not be allowed by pupils or adults within the school. A group of young men who took part in consultations as part of the Health Education Authority campaign development described how teachers would sometimes tease them about growing facial hair or their voice breaking (Blake 1999). Even though it was done light-heartedly, they felt undermined and felt that it signalled to peers that it was OK to tease each other. Similarly, girls and young women often report being teased by boys and young men about menstruation (Prendergast 1994). Girls and young women need easy access to sanitary products, to be able to leave the classroom easily and adequate sanitary product disposal facilities.

Asking for help

A school needs to foster an overall culture where asking for help is welcomed and rewarded. Pupils need to be aware of whom they can seek help from on issues to do with relationships and sexual health within the school and the community. This means teachers need to be skilled and confident in offering support and must be knowledgeable about school and community-based 'help' services.

Giving pupils a voice

Article 12 of the UN Convention on the Rights of the Child (UNCRC) states that 'children should be given opportunities to express their views on decisions that affect their lives.' The UK Government has signed up to the UNCRC. The Sex Education Forum and the National Children's Bureau believe that pupils' involvement is key to improving health and education outcomes for children. There is a culture developing within England of finding out what children and young people want and need by involving and consulting them. This is demonstrated at government level in the publication of the *Core principles for consulting with and involving children and young people* (Children and Young People's Unit 2001) and the development of young people's advisory forums such as the groups advising the Teenage Pregnancy Strategy, Quality Protects and the Children and Young People's Unit.

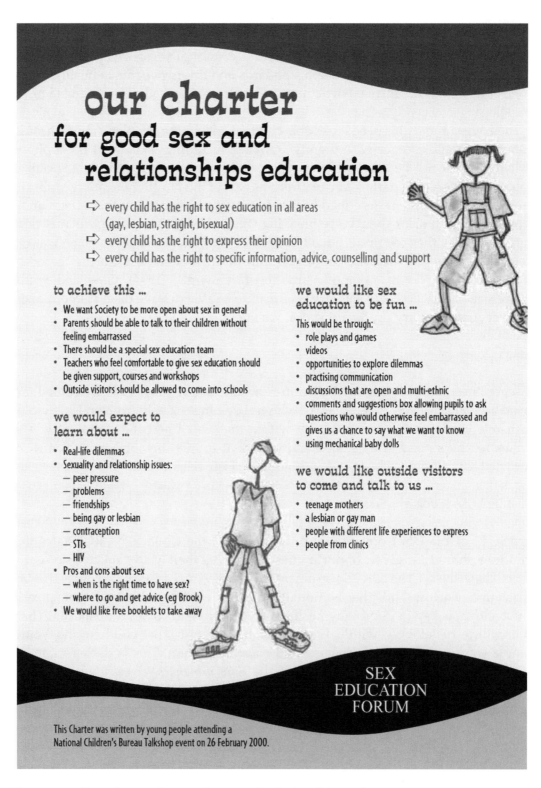

Figure 3.3 Our charter for good sex and relationships education

The Sex Education Forum regularly consults with children and young people to ascertain their views and ideas for improving SRE. They produced the following Charter for effective sex and relationships education, shown in Figure 3.3. This could be photocopied or downloaded from the SEF website and used as a basis for discussion with other pupils, school governors, the staff team and parents, carers and the wider community.

A video *Sex, Relationships, Myths and Education: Young People Talking about SRE* has also been produced (see Resources list, p. 118). This can be used in consultation as part of policy and practice development or as part of a training session.

At local authority level there are youth forums or councils.

Preston Youth Forum presented to the local healthy school conference about the importance of children and young people's participation. They highlighted that:

- If children and young people participate, it is more likely they will feel engaged with learning.
- If you consult them, feed back any action quickly so that they know what is happening.
- If you don't want to hear the views, please don't ask for them as it is worse not to be listened to when you have been asked than not to be asked in the first place.

At school level, formal opportunities for participating in SRE might be offered through developing a school council, enabling pupils to develop skills as peer supporters or peer educators and through one-off events or conferences.

One school has developed a school health council in response to pupils' wishes.

A group of pupils at a school in Greenwich were interested in health and set up a sub-group of the school council to address health issues within the school. The group developed their own agenda, carried out surveys about aspects of health education and fed their ideas and views back to the school council.

Pupils influencing planning

Identifying pupils' needs to inform curriculum planning is essential. Time and again pupils say that SRE is not relevant to them and when they are asked for their views, it can then meet their needs. Too often, SRE is based on adult agendas of what we think they should learn, rather than what they feel is relevant.

> Redbridge LEA and the Sex Education Forum consulted a group of primary school children on SRE. Pupils were consulted in class groups. They demonstrated an in-depth understanding of the complexity of relationships and importantly discussed the range of sources of information about sex and relationships. They described chain text messaging as a way of gaining information. The 'data' was then used to inform lesson planning.

> Health Promotion in Norfolk carried out a consultation conference with over 90 young people to ascertain their views and ideas for SRE. A questionnaire asking for their ideas and views formed part of the event. This has now been analysed and a video of the event has been made to inform presentations in local schools and services to improve school-based SRE and service provision.

Provision of pupils' support services

> *It's really hard if people don't know where to go to get help.*
> *(young woman, aged 14)*

> *We need to know where to go and who we can talk to.*
> *(young man, aged 13)*

The classroom is a public place and therefore it is not appropriate for pupils to ask personal questions or seek advice there. All primary, secondary and special schools need to ensure that pupils have adequate support and information about support services within the school and the wider community. Formal curriculum lessons need to support pupils in developing the skills to access these services. The SRE *Guidance* (0116/2000) clearly states: 'young people need access to, and precise information about, confidential contraceptive information, advice and services' (2000: 18). The Ofsted report on SRE (2002) highlights the importance of pastoral support and links into the community. The report emphasises the importance of effective referral systems and sensitivity in the arrangements.

Peer supporters, school counsellors, Connexions advisers, school nurses, youth workers and other community services including telephone helplines provide information and support for pupils.

When asked about advertising sexual health services, a group of young people at a Further Education College suggested:

- Posters should be in a public place to help make it alright.
- Posters should be in a semi-private place so we can take down the information.
- Posters should be in a very private place such as school diaries so we can all get the information without asking for it.

A group of young men, when asked about posters, said, 'Remember to make the writing big so we don't have to get up close to get the number!' (Blake 1999).

Pupils can make posters about their local services as part of an art and citizenship project.

> Pupils in a school in south London found out about local and national help and advice services and then developed a series of posters that were displayed on the school notice board.

> North West Lancashire Health Promotion worked with primary school children to make posters about bullying and getting help. The posters have been published and are displayed in schools and community settings.

> Building Bridges is a project run by Working with Men, piloted in Bristol, targeting young men in the school setting. As part of the SRE programme the young men are taken to visit a sexual health service. In preparation and follow-up they are encouraged to identify how to find out about services, what would stop them accessing them and the development of skills to help them access the service.

> East Kent Community Health Trust worked with pupils to develop leaflets, posters and 'credit cards' giving details of the sexual health clinics in the local area. Some schools display the posters in the common room, and others provide the leaflets in the school common room.

> A school nurse in Bath has worked with parents, pupils and teachers to establish an agreed system for helping young people get access to contraception services at the local general practice. Meetings with parents were held to secure support for the work. Young people can ask the school nurse to make an emergency appointment for them and they are taken to the local GP.

In some areas, particularly rural areas, pupils may not be able to access services outside of the school day. School-based provision is particularly important for these pupils.

> Paignton Community College runs a service on-site, Tic-Tac. Following extensive consultation with all members of the school community this multi-disciplinary centre offers a confidential service for pupils and they can access help and support on all sorts of issues including contraception.
>
> This service has been highlighted in both the Independent Advisory Group on Teenage Pregnancy First Annual Report (2001) and the Ofsted Report (2002) as an example of excellent practice.

Staff professional development needs, health and welfare

Professional development opportunities help teachers feel confident and competent in SRE. Children and young people offered the following views about a good SRE teacher:

They need to be strict, but kind and make it fun. (girl, aged 10)

Teachers need to be trained so that they feel comfortable and we can feel comfortable talking to them about it. (young woman, aged 15)

A good teacher in general should be able to teach sex education because the same way an English teacher can take a piece of Shakespeare and make you understand and develop skills in that area, the same way a Maths teacher can teach trigonometry and algebra they should apply the same rules to sex education. (young woman, aged 14)

As with all areas of the curriculum, teachers need to be confident about both the methods that are being used and the content. Pupils do not expect teachers to know everything about sex, relationships and sexual health; they are more interested in the skills of the teacher in creating a safe environment and facilitating the class to have thoughtful, open and honest discussions.

The following list of skills and qualities was devised by a group of young people aged 11–15 at a Sex Education Forum and National Children's Bureau Talkshop. They were asked to describe 'a good sex education teacher'.

What we need from a good sex education teacher . . .

Principles
They should apply the same principles to sex education as they would in any other area of the curriculum!

Mr/s Trustworthy-open-minded-confident-considerate

Personality and other qualities
Not serious
Someone who gives respect
Be able to listen
Skilled to a certain extent
Easy to talk to
Does not dictate to the student but gives advice
Ready to help others, and give answers to the full!
Can express themselves well and in great depth
Willing to help pupils understand more about sex if they were unsure or had no knowledge

---

Some knowledge
Give clear unbiased information that is detailed
Somebody who can give advice although they may not have gone through that situation

Trust
Can be spoken to confidentially
Someone who doesn't gossip
Understand the pupils' situation and will try to be open and discreet with the information they receive
Sense of trust

Open-mindedness
Guts to answer any type of question that is asked
Upfront and can speak openly
Looks at both sides
Has great respect for others' views
Sensitivity to other people's feelings and views
Fully understands young people's needs
Not expecting too much!!

Good role model
A positive person
Happy person
Confident about what they are teaching
Role model who can be looked up to!!
Someone who can easily gain respect from a group of pupils
Someone who young people can empathise with
A good person
Is not an extra (ordinary??) human being

Partnerships with parents, carers and local communities

I don't think that it should be left to just the parents or just the school. I think it needs to be a partnership. (young woman, aged 14)

The SRE *Guidance* highlights the importance of working with parents, carers and the wider community. Their involvement in policy and practice development will:

• Improve confidence in school-based SRE and help them understand the importance of SRE in children's and young people's personal, social development. It will also ensure they are confident SRE is developed within a positive values framework that respects different faith and cultural perspectives.

- Ensure effective home, school and community links so that parents and carers can reinforce learning within the home or care setting and community settings.
- Enhance the SRE programme by contributing to the curriculum by, for example, talking about having or caring for a baby, about doing particular jobs, etc. (if communities do participate in delivering aspects of SRE they, like professionals, need to work within the school values framework).

The Parents Project in Sheffield is a group of volunteer parents who have trained as peer educators. They go into schools and talk to other parents about SRE. This approach has been incredibly successful as a form of consultation. They also deliver sessions to parents about talking to their children about sex and relationships. For further information contact the Centre for HIV and Sexual Health 0114 226 1900.

Bradford Local Education Authority, Bradford Interfaith Education Centre and the Sex Education Forum held a community-based meeting that explored the role and purpose of SRE. Participants were invited through the local SACRE group.

The event was held at the Inter faith Education Centre in Bradford and representatives from the major faiths in Bradford attended. A short presentation outlining the different elements and breadth of SRE was offered followed by an opportunity to explore ideas and concerns about SRE. This meeting has been followed by a further multi-agency group meeting to identify how the LEA can support schools to deliver SRE that takes account of the issues raised and ensures children's entitlement to SRE. For further information contact the Sex Education Forum 020 7843 6056.

Assessing, recording and reporting pupils' achievement

Ofsted identified assessing and monitoring pupils' learning as an area that needs further development. Although there are no statutory assessment requirements, Ofsted's suggested learning outcomes for SRE across each of the primary and secondary phases (2002) provides a positive framework on which effective assessment of knowledge, skills and attitudes can be built. Both pupils and teachers should be involved in monitoring and assessing learning. Assessment is undertaken in relation to clear targets that are set for pupils in PSHE and Citizenship.

Schools are required to keep records on all aspects of pupils' development and annual school reports should include a section on PSHE and Citizenship. If pupils keep a record of their progress, reporting on this aspect of the curriculum will be more effective.

Pupils can undertake a range of activities that forms the basis of assessment. Where possible, material can form the basis of a portfolio to record progress. Pupils can undertake a range of individual, small and whole group activities. These include:

- planning a talk, a presentation, leading a discussion or debate, or leading an assembly;
- evidence of planning a visit or arranging for a speaker;
- completing sentence stems such as 'I was surprised that ...', I learnt that ...';
- taking part in a quiz or questionnaire;
- drawing pictures or posters or designing leaflets;
- writing letters or articles for school or community papers;
- devising a quiz or game;
- producing a diary;
- demonstrating skills through role play;
- word storming;
- interviews and focus groups;
- drawing and writing techniques.

Monitoring and assessment are important because for pupils they form an important part of the learning process. Asking questions will help pupils to assimilate and understand what they have learnt and to identify future learning needs. Questions might include:

- What new information have you learnt today?
- What new skills have you practised or learnt?
- What do you now think or believe?
- What did it feel like to do that exercise?
- What was it like to hear different people's views?
- Did anything surprise you?
- What else do you need to know?

A Pupil Referral Unit in South Wales undertook a series of sessions on sexually transmitted infections, HIV and contraception. To review the learning small groups designed leaflets and posters emphasising the importance of safer sex and contraception use. These were then displayed within the centre. The process of making and displaying the posters and leaflets reinforced the learning and supported the development of teamwork skills and self-esteem.

For teachers, assessment provides an opportunity to ensure that:

- The learning objectives have been achieved.
- Future learning needs arising from the session are addressed.
- Planning for future years takes account of feedback.

The following self-reflection questions will be helpful for teachers in identifying future learning needs and reflecting on what they did well and what they might want to change:

- What skills did they learn?
- What new information have they learnt? How do you know they have learnt it?
- What do they now think, feel and believe?
- Did everyone engage in the activity?
- Did everyone have the opportunity to achieve at their own level?
- What do they need to learn next?
- What did you do well?
- What did you not do so well?
- What might you change next time?

Feedback should be attached to the lesson plan for future work and returned to members of staff involved in planning and delivering future SRE.

St Luke's Special School in Hertfordshire was a prizewinner of the Pamela Sheridan Award for Sex Education in 2001. They record pupils' progress using art, including photographs of activities, and written work. These files are then used to revisit and reinforce learning and as evidence of their development. The school also submitted these files as part of their evidence to their local Healthy Schools Programme.

King Edward VII School in Sheffield has an assessment policy for PSHE and Citizenship. It states that 'Assessment is varied'. It includes:

- teacher observation;
- student self-assessment;
- peer assessment e.g during role play or first aid scenarios;
- group work feedbacks;
- written key words assessment;
- formal, e.g. written assessment at end of year 9 unit of work on illegal drugs;
- games as assessment of knowledge gained e.g. Drugs card game, Who's most at risk?, STIs card game, etc.

Useful comments in teacher's mark book, records of assessment and portfolios of each individual student's work aid monitoring, progress and continuity. The current assessment policy is under review as recommendations of assessment for Citizenship and PSHE are examined to see what will best meet the needs of the school and department.

Here are some examples of pupil assessment of learning on homosexuality. Pupils were provided with sentence stems (highlighted in bold).

I feel that the work made me realise how terrifying homophobic bullying can be. It also made me realise that there is a wide range of characters and personalities who are homosexual as there are in people who are heterosexual.

. . . what we have done on sexuality has changed my views about gays but it still hasn't persuaded me to think being gay is right.

I learned that there are lots of myths surrounding gays which are all complete rubbish. I also learned that gays are just like other people.

. . . that some people who I thought I knew well have very different views from me on the subject of homosexuality.

I didn't understand why I was so against homosexuals.

. . . at first why we had to do this topic. Now I don't understand why other schools don't do this topic – it's really important and could affect the quality of people's lives.

I was surprised that many people in the class took this issue more seriously than any other issue that we have done in PSE.

. . . that the people who came in were gay because I thought you could tell when someone was gay. You can't!

I liked the group discussions the best because you challenge people who are homophobic.

. . . the video *Beautiful Thing* as it was just a nice video as all it was was a romantic tale of two people realising their love for each other. However, the only difference was that they were gay.

In future I hope this work starts in year 8.

. . . I hope to live in a world where gay people and 'straights' can be treated equally.

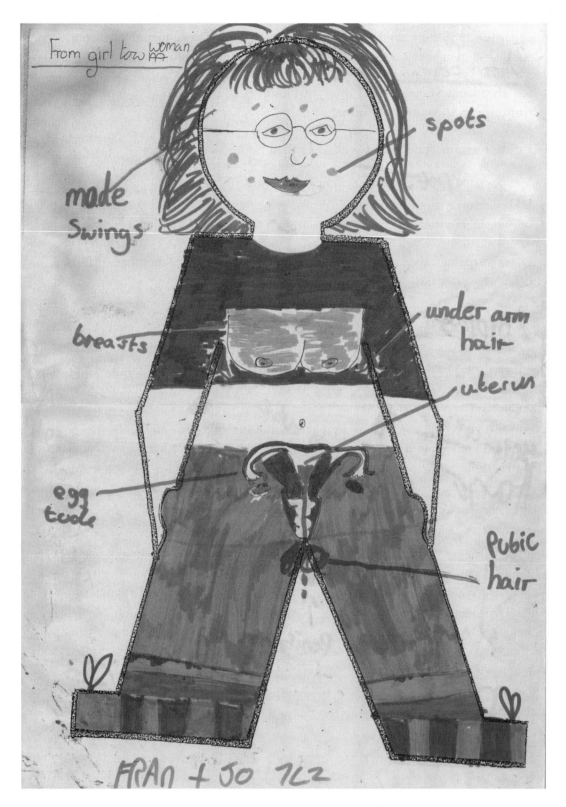

Figure 3.4 formed part of assessment of learning about the physical and emotional changes in puberty and adolescence at King Edward VII School.

4 Meeting the particular needs of all children and young people

It's a world in which everything goes and everyone has got to have a chance in it.
(young woman, aged 15)

Children's and young people's identities are shaped by a number of different factors such as gender, sexuality, race and ethnicity. This chapter explores some of the issues and particular needs of some pupils that need to be considered in the planning and delivery of SRE.

The evidence base for SRE highlights the importance of SRE being an entitlement for all as well as being targeted at marginalised pupils. An anti-discriminatory approach to the work means that some people require extra attention or resources or a different way of working to meet their needs. As well as their mainstream entitlement, some children and young people may need extra attention in order to help them manage their relationships and sexual health.

Inequalities is a term to describe differences in 'healthiness' between those at the top and those at the bottom of the social scale. The government is committed to reducing health inequalities and has set targets to do this. Education plays a role in helping to reduce these inequalities.

Inclusion is a term used in relation to education. In this context it is concerned with securing an environment and curriculum that are relevant and accessible for all members of the school community.

General tips for being inclusive are:

- Don't make assumptions about faith-based or cultural practices.
- Don't assume all young people or their carers are heterosexual. Use terms like partners or carers.
- Don't use language that perpetuates prejudice. Ensure that language used across the school is congruent with all curriculum-based SRE.
- Do discuss the effects of prejudice and discrimination faced by men and women, gay and bisexual men and women, black and Asian people and people with disabilities and impairments.
- Do ensure that racism, sexism, misogyny, homophobia and all other types of bullying, prejudice and violence are challenged at all times.
- Do ensure that discussions and images in resources reflect the diversity of the group and community.

Gender

Boys, if they have slept with someone, they get a pat on the back and it's good. If girls, they generally, um, people tend to think, they don't think very highly if a girl has slept with someone. (young woman, aged 15)

Being a boy or a girl plays a key role in all of our interactions and relationships. Our understanding of gender and what it means to be a man or a woman plays a significant part in what we expect from relationships and how we are within them. Research shows that gender has a huge impact upon the negotiation of safer sex and relationships (Holland *et al.* 1998; Adams 2002).

We are living in a period of rapid change; children and young people are experiencing conflicting messages about gender roles and identity. There is often a huge conflict between traditional gender stereotypes and the popular media claims of 'girl power' and 'new men', and their own experiences of growing up.

Single gender sessions that enable pupils to think about gender, sexuality and relationships can be helpful in providing varied learning opportunities and helps create a safe environment.

A school in Gwent offered boys and girls the opportunity to think about gender and sexuality as part of their PSHE and Citizenship programme. Boys and girls were split into single gender groups prior to a half-day event. In their single gender groups they were asked to consider the different societal expectations of men and women; what they would like to change and to identify any issues that they would like to think about or explore with the opposite sex.

Each group devised a list of issues that they would like to discuss and think about in relation to gender. Teachers and pupils then worked together to plan how they would like to run the study day. The activities were structured so that boys and girls went into mixed gender groups of six. They each had the opportunity to discuss and record their answers before joining a whole group plenary to identify key learning points. The recorded discussions were then used to form the basis of a school display exploring gender stereotyping.

Ethnicity, faith and culture

It [SRE] needs to take account of different cultural beliefs.
(young woman, aged 13)

SRE needs to be sensitive to and mindful of different cultures and faiths. Pupils with a faith or cultural tradition need to feel as though they are affirmed and respected in their beliefs and values. Pupils also need to develop an understanding of the diversity of lifestyles, beliefs and practices. Promoting one lifestyle or set of beliefs is not good practice. Pupils need to learn to respect the differences between people. This means that during discussions about sex and relationships the range of religious and secular perspectives are included and valued.

The Race Relations Amendment Act (2000) requires that all schools work towards promoting racial equality. A guide for schools published by the Commission for Racial Equality (2002) is currently out for consultation. It highlights the importance of an environment and curriculum that are relevant for all pupils and promote racial harmony. Children and young people from black and ethnic minority groups often experience implicit and explicit racism and suffer disproportionately from sexual ill health.

SRE needs to provide an opportunity to explore different cultural values and beliefs and resources need to be representative of different races and cultures.

Children and young people with HIV

With advances in combination therapy, more and more children who are infected with HIV will live into adolescence and adulthood and consequently are likely to develop sexual relationships. They therefore need to be equipped to manage their relationships and their sexual health.

Recent research (Lewis 2001) has indicated that children and young people living with (infected and affected by) HIV are dissatisfied with the sex and relationships education they receive at schools. They said that they had received little or no education which covered HIV in sufficient depth and that schools need to set more time aside for SRE. They identified that schools need to 'be more aware that there may be young people infected or affected with HIV/AIDS in the classroom during such lessons and this could impede their involvement' (Lewis 2001: 134). Children and adults with HIV still experience prejudice and discrimination and SRE has a role to play in challenging the prejudice and stigma surrounding HIV.

Lesbian, gay and bisexual children and young people

Prejudice is based on ignorance and we need to be taught about it so we do not have prejudice in our society. (young man, aged 14)

Growing up lesbian or gay can be a frightening and lonely experience. Many young people experience bullying and rejection from their peers (Forrest *et al.* 1997) as well as from adults (Lenderyou and Ray 1997). In a national survey of lesbians and gay men, it was revealed that:

- 90 per cent had been called names;
- 61 per cent had been harassed;
- 48 per cent had been violently attacked;
- 22 per cent had been beaten up.

About half of the violent attacks were perpetrated in school by their peers (Mason and Palmer 1996).

Addressing homosexuality in SRE is important because:

- All young people, regardless of their sexuality, need to know and understand about homosexuality to reduce prejudice and misunderstanding.
- Young gay and lesbian pupils need to feel supported and affirmed in their identity and to receive sexual health information that will help them manage their relationships and sexual health.
- SRE should challenge prejudice and homophobia.
- SRE has a role in framing sexuality, sexual identity and sexual orientation in a positive light.
- Exploration of attitudes and values towards sex, sexuality and relationships is an integral part of SRE.

There is a tendency to separate homosexuality within SRE and either not talk about it at all or do one lesson about homosexuality. This gives the impression that homosexual and heterosexual relationships are innately different and, indeed, that the type of sexual activity is also different.

While explicit lessons exploring prejudice including homophobia are helpful, it is important to integrate discussion about different sexualities throughout the course. Language is incredibly powerful and can make the difference in a pupil feeling validated and affirmed or feeling excluded. When talking about relationships refer to partners, instead of boyfriend or girlfriend. When talking about sex, talk about anal, oral and vaginal sex rather than foreplay and sex.

Children and young people with a disability

Disabilities can be sensory, physical or learning. The type of disability will affect the methodologies used to ensure effective learning. Chapter 7 looks at the needs of pupils with learning disabilities in particular.

Children and young people with a disability are in need of particular attention because of:

- denial of their sexuality and prejudice towards people with a disability;
- lack of social opportunities available to them to develop interpersonal and sometimes sexual relationships. This therefore means that there is not access to a friendship network where young people work out and learn about sex and relationships;
- lack of appropriate sexual health education and support that many experience in both mainstream and special education;
- lack of accessible services and adequately trained staff;
- lack of appropriate resources for people with a range of physical, learning and sensory impairments;
- their vulnerability to sexual abuse.

Disabled children and young people have the same entitlement to education as their non-disabled peers. With more disabled pupils attending mainstream schools, it is imperative that SRE takes account of their needs. There is anecdotal evidence that some pupils with disabilities in mainstream schools are being removed from PSHE to focus on literacy and numeracy. This is unacceptable. The section on differentiated learning on p. 39 gives some strategies for ensuring the range of abilities within a group are catered for.

Children and young people with disabilities are a diverse group and there is a need to think creatively and broadly and respond appropriately to the range of impairments and disabilities that children and young people have. For example, children and young people with a learning disability may need particular support in issues of public and private; children and young people with a visual impairment need education and support which enables them to physically touch objects such as model penises; and children with a physical disability that requires intimate care may need particular help and support in claiming a sense of rights over their bodies.

Children and young people excluded from school

Children and young people who are excluded from school are vulnerable to poor sexual health and early pregnancy. They will have experienced difficulties with relationships and therefore will need extra work to help them develop the personal and social skills to form positive relationships and manage their sexual health.

Children and young people in care

Children and young people in care may already have experienced many traumatic events including neglect, and sexual, physical and emotional abuse, often perpetrated by their parents and carers (Patel Kanwal and Frances-Lenderyou 1998). This can distort their understanding of sex, sexuality and personal relationships. Research indicates that there is a complex and interlinked set of risk-taking behaviour involving running away, misuse of drugs and alcohol, unsafe sex and sexual exploitation, involvement in prostitution and other offending behaviour. These may all be external symptoms of low self-esteem and emotional distress. SRE can address some of these issues but it is likely that extra support will be necessary.

In each school there is a designated teacher to support the education of children in care who may be able to offer extra support on sex and relationships issues outside of the school curriculum. Some areas have a designated nurse for Looked After Children who may also be able to offer extra support and a link to sexual health services.

Children and young people who have been sexually abused

Young people who have been sexually abused need additional attention if they are to make sense of the damaging experiences and develop a positive understanding of sex and sexuality. In any classroom there is the possibility that a pupil will have been sexually abused. Often teachers do not know about the abuse. Care therefore needs to be taken to ensure that assumptions are not made. For example, sex is not always a choice and this needs to be acknowledged. When talking about sexual activity, be clear that sex should ALWAYS be consensual. If people hurt or abuse others, it is wrong and it is not the abused person's fault. Good SRE that offers these types of messages may lead to disclosure that must then be addressed within the child protection framework of the school.

The role modelling of the teacher in maintaining boundaries and talking about sex and relationships in a positive and respectful way is fundamental. This will include, where the abuse is known, discussing when and whether the pupil attends school-based SRE. In addition to school-based SRE, pupils who have been sexually abused will require extra support. A range of professionals including staff from social services can offer this type of support.

5 Sex and relationships education in the primary school

SRE at primary school is often carried out under a number of different subject headings including

- Growing up
- Our bodies
- Personal relationships education
- My body.

SRE at the primary phase is crucial in enabling children to learn about the world around them and develop the skills to be emotionally resourceful. In addition children learn about gender and relationships from an early age by watching the world around them and from informal sources including friends and TV. Much of this information is incorrect and confusing.

Consultations with primary school children demonstrate the complexity of their understanding. Boys and girls were consulted as part of a recent primary school development project. They described how worrying growing up can be if you don't have enough information. They also described the diversity of places they had picked up information about sex, such as messages advertising sex in phone boxes, the graffiti on the bridge at the canal and the things that their parents and family had told them during separation and divorce situations (Jolly *et al.* forthcoming 2002). Without formal SRE, children continue the process of learning about sex and relationships unguided and unsupported (Collyer 1995).

The whole-school ethos supports children's personal and social development and provides a safe and supportive context for SRE. Consulting with children about what they need and want is an important part of helping them develop responsibility and decision-making skills. A group of children in a London school have been working on their PSHE and Citizenship curriculum by consulting with their peers and parents about the content. When asked about the experience they replied, 'It is really good to feel as though you are making a difference. We had lots of decisions to make.' This emphasises that the process of developing SRE as part of PSHE and Citizenship is as important as the curriculum content.

Children need to know there are clear parameters around acceptable and unacceptable behaviour in relation to difference and harassment. Children's bodies will begin to develop and change while they are at primary school and it is important that they feel supported through puberty. For girls there needs to be easily accessible sanitary facilities and all children need private changing facilities.

The early spoken and unspoken messages play an important part in developing children's values. If they are unchallenged, the primary school supports and colludes with the development of negative attitudes including sexism, racism and homophobia. This was demonstrated by consultations carried out with boys using draw and write techniques as part of the Forum project aiming at improving SRE for boys and young men. Their responses showed that from a very early age, as young as 4 or 5, they have taken on messages about how to be a man as well as messages about things that are considered girly. Girls were also considered to be silly.

By Key Stage 2, the boys had already learnt that being gay was a negative thing and giggled about being gay. The 10- and 11-year-old boys were asked what is good about having boyfriends. They replied: 'It is OK to have friends who are boys, but you do not call them boyfriends because boys who have boyfriends are gay' (Wild 1997).

The organisation of PSHE and Citizenship

At the Foundation Stage and at Key Stage 1 SRE is the responsibility of the class teacher who will generally know each child and often their parents as well. Teachers are concerned about the use of language, supporting children's emotional development and their skills in forming friendships and other relationships. Teachers also need to answer all the children's questions openly and honestly. Staff meetings or an INSET session with the LEA PSHE Advisory Teacher or Healthy Schools team, the school nurse or another health professional can help promote an agreed approach to these issues.

In Key Stage 2 more formal SRE includes preparation for puberty. An understanding of conception and birth as a minimum for SRE will generally be the responsibility of the class teacher. In many local authorities, where there is a school nursing service, team teaching is an effective approach, particularly where the school nurse supports the teacher in planning and methodology. The school nurse and other visitors provide an opportunity for single gender sessions.

Children report wanting their parents to be their first sex educator. Schools can support parents in their role as sex educators by offering them leaflets or support organisations. Parents offer support in SRE and contribute to the curriculum by talking about parenting, for example, by bringing a younger sibling into the classroom. This type of input needs to be carefully planned.

As outlined in Chapter 2, effective policy underpins good classroom practice. In particular, primary school policies need to explicitly support teachers and visitors in answering questions that children ask. The policy will need to outline what teachers should do if a pupil says they are sexually active. This would be a child protection issue.

Increasingly, children with special needs are attending mainstream school and the policy needs to specifically address how the particular needs of these children are met.

Participation and peer support

Children's participation in all aspects of school life develops self-esteem and their ability to work together positively in a school community. Developing structures with children where they help and support others offers children the opportunity to experience positive relationships with their peers and to gain personal and social skills that are an integral part of SRE. Further information on peer support can be found by visiting the Peer Support Forum website www.ncb.org.uk/psf.htm. Peer support is often used to help children in the transition from primary to secondary school. Pupils from secondary schools are 'buddied' with pupils from the primary school to provide support as they make the move.

Boys and girls learning together

Evidence from The Netherlands suggests that the way boys and girls interact with each other may be a significant factor in the improved relationships and lower teenage pregnancy rates (Ingham 1998). The evidence suggests that boys and girls continue to learn and talk with each other, enabling the development of empathy and respect. In the UK boys and girls tend to split into single sex groups from a very early age and then may not come together again until they have sexual relationships during adolescence. The primary school is a key setting in which boys and girls can be encouraged to learn from and about each other. This supports the development of positive relationship skills.

Developmentally appropriate SRE

SRE builds on the early learning goals for the Foundation stage. The Foundation stage builds the emotional and social skills of children. SRE needs to start where the children are at and, while there is a core of skills, beliefs and knowledge that children need to learn, when and how they learn this will vary according to each class of children.

At this stage it is important that children have opportunities to develop emotionally and are able to use their emotions and their thinking skills to guide positive behaviour. This means being able to name and recognise their feelings and understand how to use their feelings and thinking skills to guide their behaviour as well as recognise the impact of their behaviour on others.

Suggested learning outcomes

At the primary level there is an integrated framework for PSHE and Citizenship within the National Curriculum. Using this as a planning framework it is intended that children do the following:

- develop confidence and make the most of their abilities;
- prepare to play an active role as citizens;

- develop a healthier, safer life style;
- develop good relationships and respect the differences between people.

At primary school SRE contributes to the foundation of PSHE and Citizenship by ensuring that all children:

- develop confidence in talking, listening and thinking about feelings and relationships;
- are able to name parts of the body and describe how their bodies work;
- can protect themselves and ask for help and support;
- are prepared for puberty.

DfEE Guidance (0116/2000: 19)

Ofsted (2002) develops this further and suggests that the following criteria might be used to assess pupils' knowledge, understanding, skills, attitudes and beliefs in relation to aspects of SRE. Those marked with an * are part of the National Curriculum Science requirements.

By the end of Key Stage 1

Pupils will be able to do the following:

- recognise and compare the main external parts of the bodies of humans*;
- recognise similarities and differences between themselves and others and treat others with sensitivity*;
- identify and share feelings with others;
- recognise safe and unsafe situations;
- identify and be able to talk with someone they trust;
- be aware that their feelings and actions have an impact on others;
- make a friend, talk with them and share feelings ;
- use simple rules for dealing with strangers and for resisting pressure when they feel safe unsafe and uncomfortable.

Pupils will know and understand:

- that animals, including humans, grow and reproduce*;
- that humans and animals can produce offspring and these grow into adults*;
- the basic rules for keeping themselves safe and healthy;
- about safe places to be and safe people to be with;
- the needs of babies and young people;
- ways in which they are like and different from others;
- they have control over their actions and bodies;
- the names of the main external parts of the body including agreed names for sexual parts;
- why families are special for caring and sharing.

Pupils will have given thought to the following:

- why families are special;
- the similarities and differences between people;
- how their feelings and actions have an impact on other people.

By the end of key stage 2

Pupils will be able to do the following:

- express opinions, for example, about relationships and bullying;
- listen to and support others;
- respect other people's viewpoints and beliefs;
- recognise their changing emotions with regard to friends and family and be able to express their feelings positively;
- identify adults they can trust and ask for help;
- be self-confident in a wide range of new situations e.g. seeking new friends;
- form opinions that they can articulate to a variety of audiences;
- recognise their own worth and identify positive things about themselves;
- balance the stresses of life in order to promote their own mental health and well-being and that of others;
- see things from other people's viewpoints, for example, their parents' and their carers';
- discuss moral questions;
- listen to and support their friends and manage friendship problems;
- recognise and challenge stereotypes, for example, in relation to gender;
- recognise the pressure of unwanted physical contact and know ways of resisting it.

Pupils will know and understand:

- that the life processes common to humans and other animals include growth and reproduction*;
- about the main stages of the human life cycle*;
- that safe routines can stop the spread of viruses including HIV;
- about the physical changes that take place at puberty, why they happen and how to manage them, e.g. periods and wet dreams;
- the many relationships in which they are all involved;
- where individual families and groups can find help;
- how the media impact on forming attitudes;
- about keeping themselves safe when involved in risky activities;
- that their actions have consequences and be able to anticipate the results of them;
- about different forms of bullying people and the feelings of both bullies and victims;
- why being different can provoke conflict and why this is unacceptable;
- about and accept a wide range of different family arrangements, for example, marriage, second marriages, fostering, step-brothers and step-sisters and half-brothers and half-sisters, extended families and three or more generations living together.

Pupils will have given thought to:

- diversity of life styles;
- others' points of view, including their parents';
- why being different can provoke bullying and why this is unacceptable;
- when it is appropriate to take a risk and when to say no and seek help;
- the diversity of values and customs in the school and in the community;
- the need for trust and love in relationships.

Children's knowledge can be assessed using a variety of methods including draw and write activities, questionnaires, pupil surveys and discussion activities. Word storming activities also offer a starting point for assessing children's levels of knowledge and understanding and can help teachers understand how to approach a topic.

Specific issues

Teaching about puberty – boys and girls

Children must know and understand about the physical and emotional changes that take place during puberty *before* it happens. Too often children report that they did not get information until after they had started puberty.

Both genders need to know and understand the changes that take place for girls and for boys. Although some learning about puberty may be done in single sex groups, it is important that each covers the basic information about themselves and the opposite gender and they develop the skills to talk to each other. Girls often report being teased by boys about menstruation (Prendergast 1994). A group of 15-year-old boys were asked why they thought boys might tease girls about menstruation. After some intense discussion they agreed that they did not understand menstruation and if boys did, they might not tease girls. They thought that the teasing was probably a way of trying to find out about it.

Pubertal development, however, is much broader than menstruation. For both boys and girls it involves bodily changes including the growth of hair, greater perspiration levels, etc. Education needs to focus on these broad aspects and ensure that the different needs of children are met.

Puberty often goes unnoticed in boys or the focus is on wet dreams. Voice breaking, growing facial hair and uncontrollable erections are all issues that need to be included confidently. Many boys living without a father will not have a man who they can ask for help and information about these issues and evidence suggests that often the female carer does not know enough about boys' development (Lenderyou and Ray 1997). School, therefore, is a positive and important site for learning.

Accurate terminology

It is a requirement in Key Stage 1 that children know the main external parts of the human body. Children need to know the correct terms for the parts of the body, including the sexual parts. Many children grow up with 'family names' and pseudonyms. While it is important to mention that these names might exist, teachers use the correct name in the classroom.

Children need to be able to talk about the parts of the body in case they need to talk to adults about it, for example, if they were being hurt sexually by another child or adult.

Accurate naming is also important to ensure effective learning. They need to be offered new terms for new concepts so that they understand fully what they are being taught.

Boys often have names for the external parts of their bodies but girls less frequently have a sexual language. If they are to develop a sense of their bodies as a source of pride it is important that the clitoris is named, as well as reproductive parts of the body.

Talking about sexual behaviour, sexuality, contraception and HIV

Children often ask questions about sexual behaviour, sexuality, reproduction and disease. Honest answers are important to prevent worry and confusion and to help them understand the difference between safe touching and abusive behaviours, and to help them learn about prejudice and understand that sexual activity is a natural and pleasurable part of life.

HIV

Research has shown that very young children have heard about HIV and AIDS and much of this information is wrong, based on adult prejudice and worrying for them. Childline published a report highlighting the types of questions that children have about HIV. The report *'Can I Catch it from a Toothbrush?'* (Cross 2000) reinforced the need for accurate education about HIV and AIDS. Questions or comments about HIV may arise at unexpected moments such as when children are picking up rubbish; children may say, for example, 'We must not pick up needles'. This emphasises the importance of a clear policy framework and training for all staff involved in the school, including the midday supervisors, so that consistent messages are offered to children.

Reproduction and contraception

National Curriculum Science at Key Stage 1 requires that children develop an understanding that 'humans produce babies and these babies grow into children and then into adults'. The SRE aspects of PSHE could include work on the needs of animals and families of all kinds, people who help us and responsibilities and rights.

As children progress to Key Stage 2, the Science Curriculum requires that children are taught 'about the main stages of the life cycle'. This requires that children begin to understand about fertility and that they begin to learn about contraception. Children will often have seen contraception in the home, or heard adults talking about it, and teachers can introduce the idea that adults can decide whether or not to have a baby.

Homosexuality

All children need to be prepared to live in an increasingly diverse society that is safe for all citizens. It is the responsibility of a school to promote positive beliefs and values that support this. Homophobia, like all other forms of prejudice, needs to be challenged. Children are very familiar with the notion of homosexuality. They can develop homophobic attitudes in the primary school, particularly if expressed views go unchallenged, or they can learn that homophobia is unacceptable. There is now a range of diverse life styles and family arrangements. Some children may be living with gay parents or have gay siblings; older pupils may already be beginning to identify particular feelings and they need to feel supported and validated in the whole school and in SRE.

If questions are asked, responses such as 'sometimes two men or two women also love each other like men and women do' can be helpful in supporting children's understanding. If further questions are asked about sexual behaviour, the response could be 'like men and women, people who are gay kiss and touch each other in ways that make them feel nice'.

In many primary schools conversations and games take place that enforce a message that being gay is wrong. Examples include 'gay tag' and the 'gay line'. How this is responded to is really important. Often interventions such as 'don't be silly, of course he is not gay' take place. This reinforces the ideas that being gay is wrong or bad. It might be more helpful to say something like, 'It is not wrong or bad to be gay.'

Masturbation

Most children discover that touching their genitals gives them pleasure and yet it can be associated with guilt and dirtiness. Many myths still prevail about masturbation including that it can do harm.

Some religions and cultures forbid masturbation. Generally in our culture male masturbation is talked about much more frequently than female masturbation. Children may ask about masturbation. They need confident, honest answers.

When explaining masturbation to children it is important to emphasise that it must be done in private and that it will not do any physical harm. Respect for religious and cultural teachings is maintained by including it in the teaching and suggesting that a child talks to an adult they trust about it.

Sexual activity

Reproduction forms part of the statutory science orders and children are interested in how they arrived in the world. Adults often get nervous about talking about sex with children for fear that it will have a negative impact. Easy to understand honest answers are necessary. Children can become worried and confused if they are told stories such as the stork delivers the baby!

Explanation of sexual intercourse should be done in a way that is easy for children to understand. A positive approach would be to explain that people behave differently with different people, e.g. when you know somebody you say hello, when you care about somebody you might cuddle them.

Using this as a starting point and offering clear examples, say that sometimes when people are grown up and they love each other, they have sex with each other. They do this because it feels nice and sometimes because they want to have babies.

Methods

As well as the teaching methods outlined in Chapter 3, the following methods have been used in the primary school to great effect.

Circle time

Circle time, where children undertake planned activities in a circle, provides an opportunity to develop key relationship skills such as empathy, naming and recognising emotions, listening to the views and feelings of others and expressing their opinions. These are core emotional and social skills necessary for effective learning and interaction in the wider world.

Circle time provides a positive process through which children can learn to value the differences and similarities between themselves and others and develop co-operative ways of working together. Circle time can be based on events within the school life and can focus on particular topics chosen by adults or by the children. It needs to be flexible and responsive to children's needs.

> A first school in Milton Keynes places circle time as a key aspect of school life. Children learn to listen to each other and to offer and receive positive feedback from their peers. The children have developed a whole range of skills and importantly are confident in naming positive qualities that they and their peers have. Each child has a special day, when they are able to bring in a possession and discuss why they like it. On their special day the other children in the class all tell the child one thing that makes the person special.
>
> The teacher writes down all the reasons that the child is told they are special and gives it to the child. The children then take this home.

Fiction

There are many excellent books for children and many schools use the literacy hour to address SRE-related topics. Raising literacy levels is a key national and local priority in education and this is a positive approach to learning about relationships. Using books provides an excellent way of distancing the learning, i.e. using characters that the children can relate to without talking about their own experience. Fiction covers a wide range of topics including bereavement, bullying, separation and divorce, safety and gender roles. *Hand in Hand: Emotional Development Through Literature* (Hunter *et al.* 1998) provides suggestions for materials to support emotional development. A full list of fiction books is available on the Sex Education Forum website: www.ncb.org.uk/sef.

Puppets

Using puppets is an effective way of distancing activities. They are particularly good to use with children who have special needs to help distinguish between real and fictional characters. They are also helpful for children with low literacy levels or behavioural difficulties. Some schools have used professional puppeteers to provide sessions. Other schools have worked with the children to make the puppets. Using puppets can be a powerful tool for engaging children incredibly quickly and can often help the quieter children in the class to learn effectively. Puppets can be used to explore a wide range of issues including feelings and emotions, being special, relationships and HIV.

6 Sex and relationships education in the secondary school

SRE in the secondary school builds on the foundations that are laid in the primary school. It is developmental and progressive. Often children and young people say that SRE in the secondary school covers 'old ground' and does not provide new learning. Effective partnership with feeder schools enables this to be avoided. Working to the learning outcomes as suggested by Ofsted for primary schools (2002: 37–40) and secondary schools (2002: 40–43) ensures that SRE is continuous and progressive.

Young people in secondary schools

Young people in secondary schools are at a significant time in their developing sexuality because they are experiencing puberty, body changes and sexual desire and engaging in different sorts of relationships and sexual activity. SRE therefore supports them in managing their relationships now and developing emotional and social skills for the future.

Many young people report that SRE was not relevant and it assumed that none of them were having relationships or sex.

> *People in general tend to say, just say no, and that is basically the view that every young person grows up with, thinking, yeah, I would just say no in that situation. But when you get in a situation it is not as easy as just say no, because you can get carried away and it is not just the other person, you can get carried away as well.* (young woman, aged 15)

To be relevant, it needs to explore the reality of young people's lives. As one teacher said, 'You never know whether this is the day that they REALLY need sex education. It could be the last time they hear it.' *'They like to pretend that none of us are having sex, well some of us ARE and sex education needs to give us the information we need'* (young woman, aged 15).

Pupils will come from a wide range of backgrounds and their diverse needs will be addressed in policy and curriculum development. Increasingly pupils with special needs are in mainstream schools. Policy and practice need to explicitly address their particular needs including how they may receive extra support in SRE.

The organisation of PSHE and Citizenship

SRE in the secondary school forms part of an integrated PSHE and Citizenship. It can be organised in a range of different ways. It is not helpful for teachers with a light timetable in their subject specialism to be allocated to the PSHE and citizenship team without adequate training and support. This is not fair on either the teacher or the pupils. Poor teaching in this area of the curriculum will leave pupils without their entitlement to high quality SRE.

Ofsted (2002) confirms that teaching and learning are generally more effective where there is a specialist team, as opposed to a team of tutors. A specialist team is a team who have the qualities and competencies necessary to engage with young people and their personal and social development. Young people in secondary schools will be developing as independent young adults, with all the difficulties and joys that this involves.

How to organise a specialist team

A specialist team can be organised in a number of ways, dependent on the organisation of SRE in the curriculum.

1. Where PSHE and Citizenship is designated as a department, members of the team can each be allocated to a particular class for their PSHE and Citizenship lessons. They will be responsible for that group for the whole year and will as part of the course teach their units. The advantages of this type of organisation are that:

   (a) The teacher can develop an on-going relationship with the group, whereby trust can be established.
   (b) The emphasis can focus more on a holistic approach to personal development rather than a topic-based focus.
   (c) Pupils can be helped to work effectively with each other.

The disadvantage is that teachers have to be confident in a number of themes.

2. The PSHE and Citizenship programme most often seen at Key Stage 4 is organised on a carousel basis, where each member of the team is responsible for a different theme, for example, safety, drugs or sex and relationships. Pupils move to a different teacher at the end of each unit.
   The advantages of organising the curriculum in this way are:

   (a) Teachers can develop a theme-based specialism in which they feel confident and competent.
   (b) Pupils work with a variety of teachers.

The disadvantages are:

   (a) The focus tends to be on topic-based information rather than holistic development of personal and social skills and values clarification. This means that time may not be used to maximise pupil learning.
   (b) All units have to be the same length which is not always desirable or appropriate.

    (c) Pupils will receive the units at different times throughout the year rather than at a time when the majority are ready. For example, it is not always ideal to start with the SRE unit, before the group has established itself and its way of working.

    (d) It is difficult to establish a relationship with pupils where there is a maximum of one half term of lessons.

3. A specialist team can include staff from within the school and a range of professionals from outside the school. These professionals team-teach with teachers who may not feel competent or comfortable with SRE, for example, with tutors who deliver SRE as part of a tutor-led approach. In some schools a specialist SRE teacher is attached to each year team. The advantages of this type of organisation are:

    (a) Tutors can learn from the others so they will be able to develop their skills and competence.

    (b) Pupils may enjoy working with outside visitors.

    (c) Pupils benefit from the expertise and ease of the specialist.

The disadvantages are:

    (a) SRE is seen as special, different and possibly sensitive.

    (b) Pupil–teacher relationships are limited.

    (c) The availability of outside agencies may be limited and it is probably unsustainable.

    (d) Time-tabling a support team needs careful planning and may be difficult because tutor-led programmes normally run simultaneously.

Policy

The policy should outline how SRE is organised and delivered including the resources that are going to be used and how questions will be answered. The policy also needs to identify what will happen if a pupil says that they are sexually active and must identify a clear process for supporting them to access confidential help and support from health professionals.

Suggested learning outcomes

SRE builds on the learning in the primary school. At the secondary stage it is important that young people continue to develop emotionally and are supported to use their emotions and their thinking skills to guide positive behaviour.

At the secondary level there is a framework for PSHE as well as a statutory order for Citizenship within the National Curriculum. Using this as a planning framework it is intended that children should do the following:

- develop confidence and make the most of their abilities;
- prepare to play an active role as citizens;
- develop a healthier, safer lifestyle;
- develop good relationships and respect the differences between people.

And Citizenship requires that they develop:

- knowledge and understanding about becoming informed citizens;
- skills of enquiry and communication;
- skills of participation and responsible action.

At secondary schools SRE should prepare young people for an adult life in which they can:

- develop positive values and a moral framework that will guide their judgements, decisions and behaviour;
- be aware of their own sexuality and understand human sexuality;
- understand the arguments for delaying sexual activity;
- understand the reasons for having protected sex;
- understand the consequences of their actions and behave responsibly in sexual and pastoral relationships;
- have the confidence and self-esteem to value themselves and others and have respect for individual conscience and the skills to judge the kind of relationships they want;
- communicate effectively;
- have sufficient information and skills to protect themselves and, where they have one, their partner from unwanted conceptions and sexually transmitted infections, including HIV;
- avoid being exploited or exploiting others;
- avoid being pressured into unwanted or unprotected sex;
- access confidential sexual health advice, support and if necessary treatment;
- know how the law applies to sexual relationships.

(DfEE *Guidance* 0116/2000: 20)

DfEE *Guidance* also states that 'young people need access to, and precise information about, confidential contraceptive information, advice and services' (2000: 18).

Ofsted (2002) develops this guidance further and suggests that the following learning outcomes might be used to assess pupils' knowledge, understanding, skills, attitudes and beliefs in relation to aspects of SRE. Those marked with an * are part of the National Curriculum Science requirements.

By the end of Key Stage 3

Pupils will be able to do the following:

- manage changing relationships;
- recognise the risk to personal safety in sexual behaviour and be able to make safe decisions;
- ask for help and support;
- explain the relationship between their self-esteem and how they see themselves;
- develop assertiveness skills in order to resist peer pressure and stereotyping;
- see the complexity of topical moral, social and cultural issues and be able to form a view of their own;
- develop good interpersonal skills to sustain existing relationships as they grow and change and to help them make new relationships;
- be tolerant of the diversity of personal, social and sexual preferences in relationships;
- develop empathy with the core values of family life in all its variety of forms;
- recognise the need for commitment, trust and love in meaningful relationships which may manifest themselves in a variety of forms, including marriage;
- recognise the stages of emotions in relation to loss and change caused by divorce, separation and new family members and how to manage their feelings positively.

Pupils will know and understand:

- that fertilisation in humans is the fusion of a male and female cell*;
- the physical and emotional changes that take place during adolescence*;
- about the human reproductive system, including the menstrual cycle and fertilisation*;
- how the foetus develops in the uterus*;
- how the growth and reproduction of bacteria and the replication of viruses can affect health*;
- how the media influence understanding and attitudes towards sexual health;
- how good relationships can promote mental well-being;
- the law relating to sexual behaviour of young people;
- the sources of advice and support;
- about when and where to get help, e.g. the genito-urinary medicine (GUM) clinic, etc.

Pupils will have given thought to:

- the benefits of sexual behaviour in a committed relationship;
- how they see themselves affects their self-confidence and behaviour;
- the importance of respecting difference in relation to gender and sexuality;
- how it feels to be different and discriminated against;
- issues such as the costs of early sexual activity;
- the unacceptability of prejudice and homophobic bullying;
- what rights and responsibility mean in relationships.

By the end of Key Stage 4

Pupils will be able to do the following:

- recognise the influences and pressures around sexual behaviour and respond appropriately and confidently seek professional health advice;
- manage emotions associated with changing relationships with parents and friends;
- see both sides of an argument and express and justify a personal opinion;
- have the determination to stand up for their beliefs and values;
- make informed choices about the pattern of their life style which promote well-being;
- have the confidence to assert themselves and challenge offending behaviour;
- develop quality of empathy and sympathy and the ability to respond emotionally to the range and depth of feelings within close relationships;
- work co-operatively with a range of people different from themselves.

Pupils will know and understand:

- the way in which hormonal control occurs, including the effects of the sex hormones and some medical uses of hormones, including the control and promotion of fertility*;
- the defence mechanisms of the body*;
- how sex is determined in humans*;
- how HIV and other STIs affect the body;
- the links between eating disorders and self-image and sexual activity;
- the risks of early sexual activity and the link with the use of alcohol;
- how the different forms of contraception work and where to get advice;
- the role of statutory and voluntary organisations;
- the law in relation to sexual activity for young people and adults;
- how their own identity is influenced by both their personal values and those of family and society;
- how to respond appropriately within a range of social relationships ;
- how to access the statutory and voluntary agencies which support relationships in crisis e.g. divorce and separation;
- the qualities of good parenting and its value to family life;
- the benefits of marriage or a stable partnership in bringing up children;
- the way different forms of relationship including marriage depend for their success on maturity and commitment.

Pupils will have given thought to the following:

- their developing sense of sexual identity and feel confident and comfortable with it;
- how personal, family and social values influence behaviour;
- the arguments around moral issues such as abortion, contraception, IVF treatment and the age of consent;

- the individual contributions made by partners in a sustained relationship and how these can be of joy or benefit to both;
- the consequences of close relationships, including having children, and how this will create family ties which impact on their lives and those of others.

Many of the learning outcomes outlined above can be developed within the Citizenship curriculum. At Key Stages 3 and 4 aspects of sex and relationships can be explored within Citizenship, for example:

- considering different aspects of people's identities, such as ethnicity and faith, that shape their beliefs and values in relation to sex and sexuality;
- exploring the impact of messages offered in the media about gender and sexuality;
- understanding HIV as a global issue including its economic and social impact;
- practising expressing their opinions and listening to and evaluating those of others on a range of issues such as marriage, gender roles and teenage pregnancy;
- developing empathy and understanding of different sexualities and family arrangements;
- learning to take responsibility for their own attitudes and behaviour.

Specific issues

Contraception and safer sex

SRE helps pupils learn about and understand the range of different contraceptive methods. Often pupils are taught detailed factual information about all the different types of contraception. This is unnecessary as these will be discussed when they access contraceptive and sexual health services. The focus needs to be on developing skills to talk to a partner about protecting themselves from pregnancy and sexually transmitted infections as well as accessing contraceptive and sexual health services. The emphasis needs to be on developing their motivation and confidence to protect themselves and to be able to access services.

Alcohol and drug use

I think we need to be thinking about what can happen when we get drunk so we learn not to make too many mistakes! (young man, aged 13)

Many young people report using drugs, including alcohol. This can affect the choices they make and the risks they take. SRE uses real-life scenarios and case studies to help pupils to think about the influence of alcohol and drugs on their choices and to encourage them to develop strategies for managing these risks. Alcohol and drugs are used for different reasons and with different impacts including:

- enabling something that is expected and wanted by lowering inhibitions;
- leading to unanticipated but welcome sexual activity;
- leading to unanticipated and unwanted sexual activity where alcohol is used as a strategy to coerce another person or has led to sexual activity that may or may not be viewed negatively;
- sometimes alcohol use (or drunkenness) is offered as an explanation for sexual activity that young people feel ashamed or embarrassed about (Ingham 2002).

Peer pressure

In schools when boys go back talking about what they have done with their girlfriend, etc. it kinda makes you feel why you haven't. So peer pressure and low self-esteem make you want to do what they did and so that is what forces people to have sex.
(young woman, aged 14)

Many young people talk about the role of peer pressure in making decisions about their relationships. They also talk about the costs and benefits of decision-making, and keeping face among peers can be a motivating factor that militates against positive choices. SRE explores the reality of making choices about sex and relationships. Young people find it helpful to think about and offer each other advice about what they might say in these types of situations. Using authentic scenarios can offer opportunities to develop ideas, strategies and 'scripts'.

Violence and harassment

Violence and harassment are negative for both the perpetrator and the person on the receiving end. Violence and harassment form part of many relationships, including sexual relationships. However, they remain a hidden taboo. The Sex Education Forum has received a number of calls suggesting that girls and young women may collude with or blame themselves for violent behaviour.

Helping young people to know and understand that violence and harassment of any sort are unacceptable and that these are not the responsibility of the person who is subject to violence is a central aspect of effective education about relationships. SRE helps young people to think about the consequences of harassing or being violent towards others, and helps them develop the skills and confidence to offer and gain support.

Homosexuality

Puberty, which is what we are going through, is a really difficult time anyway and
if someone feels different anyway and does not have any information about
homosexuality ... it makes it harder for them. They should really be taught about
what they can expect to be feeling and other people should be taught it is not a
problem as such, it's not an issue. (young woman, aged 14)

*I think that gay relationships should be taught in school because most people
don't know about it. (young man, aged 15)*

78

Although it might be helpful to have a specific lesson focusing on homosexuality, prejudice and discrimination, it should not be limited to this one lesson. SRE is developed in such a way that homosexuality is integrated throughout the curriculum.

A young person quoted in Rogers (1994) provides a positive list of ideas of things that could make a difference for young lesbian and gay pupils:

- open discussion of homosexuality in class – not addressed as a problem;
- open discussion of the oppression of lesbians and gays;
- role models;
- talks by ex-pupils;
- plays and books;
- teachers standing up for you;
- being taken seriously.

Exploring media messages

Negative messages about sex, gender and sexual health are prevalent in the media. The media colludes with and perpetuates myths and misinformation. The evidence base for SRE (Health Development Agency 2001) highlights the importance of developing a critical awareness of messages in the media about sex and sexuality. Pupils undertake projects that enable them to identify and clarify the types of messages in magazines, on television or in the newspapers and develop confidence in checking out with adults whether the messages are true. The adults can be asked questions such as:

- Is this true?
- How do you know whether facts are true?
- How could you check out whether these messages are accurate?

This aspect of SRE is inextricably linked to other aspects of the curriculum including Citizenship, Sociology, General Studies, English and Media Studies.

Linking to sexual health services

The SRE *Guidance* emphasises the importance of providing specific information about local sexual health services. Bulletin boards, school–home books, websites, visitors and visits, one-off events and conferences all provide opportunities to offer accurate information about where services are, what they offer and how to get there. Running mock clinics can increase the confidence and skills of pupils to access community support and advisory services.

'Mock' sexual health clinics have been provided in Lambeth, Southwark and Lewisham since 1996. Young people are introduced to local services by incorporating group clinic visits into sex education. The aim is to provide a non-threatening environment where young people can discuss sexual health and service access issues. This is achieved by demystifying the experience of accessing primary care sexual health services by demonstrating to young people the exact location, timing and type of provision of their 'local' sexual health service. Pupils meet service staff and are reassured that services are confidential. Teachers take pupils to the clinic and family planning nurses run sessions during non-client opening times.

Strong links with sexual health services can also inform planning of SRE by providing information about local trends and issues. For example, if large numbers of young women were accessing the service and testing positive for Chlamydia, this is fed back to the school so that further work on protection against sexually transmitted infections can be integrated into the curriculum

Methods

As well as the teaching methods outlined in Chapter 3, the following methods have been used in secondary schools to enhance curriculum opportunities.

Peer education

Peer education can be a helpful addition to a teacher-led programme. Peer education harnesses the positive peer influence among young people to impart clear messages about sex and relationships. It should not be seen as a substitute for a teacher-delivered programme but instead can both develop the skills and confidence of peer educators and offer alternative learning opportunities for the peer educated.

Peer educators can develop displays focusing on a particular event such as World AIDS Day, can lead assemblies, and can run group work sessions in the classroom. Peer educators will need adequate training and on-going support to carry out their role confidently and competently.

One-off events and conferences

Many schools work together to develop one-off conferences and events. They form an excellent opportunity to intensively address issues such as sexual health or gender and to invite community advisory and support services into schools. These events encourage participation and active citizenship by enabling pupils to plan, organise, prepare and evaluate the day and offer them an opportunity to engage and give feedback to local services.

7 Sex and relationships education for children and young people with learning disabilities

The term learning disabilities covers a broad spectrum of abilities and disabilities, including children and young people with severe and moderate learning disabilities, some with additional physical disabilities, profound and multiple impairments, and some with autistic tendencies. Many of these children and young people will be educated in special schools. A growing number of children and young people, especially those with physical or moderate learning disabilities, are being integrated into mainstream schools.

Whatever their disabilities, the sexual development of these children and young people generally takes place within the normal range. It is the combination of slower cognitive development with the physical and emotional development of puberty and adolescence, and the increased susceptibility to abuse that makes SRE particularly important for these children and young people. This makes it imperative that appropriate and effective methods are used to help them develop the range of personal and social skills to form effective relationships.

Persistence over the years has gained its reward. Considerable progress has been made in recognising the sexual rights of people with disabilities, hence securing SRE as an integral part of the curriculum for children and young people with disabilities, and not before time. It was the Children Act 1989 that stated that 'sexuality is one of the most important influences' on the development of children and young people – and that means all children and young people. Whatever our abilities and disabilities, we are all sexual beings. This implies that we all have similar needs and rights. Among them, for instance, the need and right:

- for information;
- for reassurance;
- for acceptance;
- for respect and dignity;
- to love and be loved;
- to have opportunities to form relationships;
- to take risks in relationships;
- and in schools, for appropriate methods to enhance learning.

For children and young people with learning disabilities schools are central in fulfilling many of these needs, both in the formal SRE curriculum and in the pastoral and extra-curricular activities that enable friendships and relationships to develop.

This chapter draws on almost two decades of work developed and carried out by Image in Action. It is written by Lorna Scott and Lesley Kerr Edwards. Image in Action works with children, young people and adults with learning disabilities and 'acknowledges the sexuality of people with disabilities, and believes that everyone has the right to information about sex regardless of gender, age, sexual preference, disability, race or religion'. Image in Action has developed a methodology based on group work, drama and active learning.

The basis of the methodology

The slower the learner, the more concrete needs to be the learning experience. Development of skills is fundamental to success. This is true, of course, for all of us. We don't learn to drive a car by being told how to do it – we have to have a go. This is why group work is of critical importance. It enables a wide range of activities to be used that provide concrete opportunities to increase knowledge and offers opportunities to practise and develop emotional and social skills as well as positive values. Children and young people with disabilities have fewer opportunities than their peers to develop these skills in social situations. This means the school has a responsibility, in partnership with parents and community partners, to create positive learning opportunities through a wide range of curricular and extra-curricular activities.

So how DO we do it?

This chapter offers principles of working in an active way with groups of children and young people with disabilities. It is followed by a curriculum plan for pupils of primary and secondary age. In one sense, there is nothing new about these methods. Many of them are outlined in Chapter 3. What is different is the purposeful way in which these activities have been put together, with a deliberate emphasis on practising skills and a particular lesson structure that aids concentration, memory and learning. This way of working encourages participation, develops creativity and allows peer learning to take place. It relies less on literacy in the form of the written word, and more on oral, visual and tactile communication. And it is fun, which makes learning memorable. Using group work methods builds confidence, co-operation and communication – the three 'Cs' of SRE. We know it works.

> *The highlight has been in being part of the pupils' growing and maturing, and gaining confidence myself.*

> *The pupils have become more confident, communicative and assertive. (teacher)*

Some essential principles

The following principles should be read in addition to those laid out in Chapter 3. Most of these would also be true for any area of the curriculum, or indeed for a successful school, but they are particularly pertinent for SRE, with all its complexities.

- Have a clear policy that makes specific reference to the types of resources that will be used, identifies the language that will be used by all staff within the school and how SRE will be organised and delivered. The policy needs to make strong links to other policies such as confidentiality and personal care.
- Pupil participation is crucial. Start with an assessment of pupils' needs and try to find out what they need and want. A group of pupils and ex-pupils from the Shepherd School in Nottingham worked with teachers to clarify what pupils need to know and learn in SRE.
- Find out what they have previously learnt and retained. Get as rounded a picture as possible, from staff, parents and carers, and other relevant people. Children and young people with severe learning disabilities can take part in a number of practical activities while staff observe to understand what they know and what they can do. Children and young people with mild and moderate learning disabilities can be given a pre-course questionnaire that staff help them complete. This can be repeated at the end of the course to assess learning.
- Careful planning includes the flexibility to respond to pupils' needs and interests.
- Start young, as soon as pupils begin school lay the foundation of basic skills and understanding. Slow learners need plenty of time, and leaving it till later will be unhelpful.
- Consider the resources to be used. Concrete learning requires visual and 3-D materials to be explicit, probably more so than in a mainstream group. Because materials need to be explicit, it is important that this is addressed within the policy.
- Use a lesson structure that is based on ritual, repetition and reinforcement – the 3Rs. Pupils feel secure with a consistent format, so that they know what to expect in each lesson. Repetition is essential to ensure that the learning is assimilated and understood. Develop effective partnerships with parents so that they have confidence in school-based SRE and can reinforce the learning in the home.
- Finally – enjoy! If we do, so will our pupils.

Planning the programme

The content of a SRE programme can be divided into six main themes:

- body parts;
- gender;
- public and private;
- feelings;
- relationships;
- life cycle.

Each of these themes can be developed at different levels over the years. In addition, there are the basic SRE skills of permission, decision-making and assertion. All of this can be covered in three main stages of work, not necessarily coinciding with age groups but rather with pupils' ability and maturity.

Laying the foundations

Whatever the pupils' age, this is where the work begins, developing basic skills like working together in a group, taking turns and encouraging self-esteem. This work needs to be structured to prepare the ground for the SRE programme.

Basic SRE work

Foundation work will continue while introducing more content areas. This is where more specific work fits in, including work on body image, gender, public and private, feelings, private body parts and the body changes at puberty and introductory work on menstruation and masturbation. The skills of decision-making and assertion begin to be developed at this stage.

Sexuality and sexual relationships

Depending on the age and abilities of the group, this is where more explicit work is covered, such as developing a language for sexual body functions including menstruation and masturbation, sexual activity and sexual relationships, sexual health, contraception, pregnancy and birth. At this level, plenty of practice is needed on basic relationship skills like giving and seeking permission, negotiation and compromise.

This programme outline is not so very different from one that might be found in mainstream curricula. Indeed, it follows similar lines to those outlined by Ofsted for primary and secondary pupils (2002). There are some areas that need particular emphasis for children and young people with learning disabilities, like learning what is appropriate in public and private places and situations, and practising assertion skills to make their wishes known. Learning how to say no and yes – and meaning it – is essential.

Active learning methods for SRE

Many of the active learning methods are outlined in Chapter 3. This section outlines additional and particular activities for children and young people with disabilities. First of all, we aim to get the group of pupils working together in a co-operative and safe way, which builds relationships, boosts confidence and helps learning to take place. We invite suggestions for ground rules for the lessons (we are told things like 'listen to other people', 'what happens in the lesson is private'). Pupils are encouraged to decide for themselves as much as possible ('which game shall we play next?'), and to take responsibility for themselves and what they do. It's important to emphasise that the work is not personal; it relies on 'distancing' techniques to keep the work safe. Sex and relationships education is intended to be just that – educational, not therapeutic.

There are some 'core' activities that can be used for SRE, listed below. Almost all effective classroom activities for SRE are a variation on one or the other of these; and with familiarity and practice it becomes easy to develop variations of our own:

Stationary circle activities
Pupils interact as a group by:

- Watching the activity.
- Following the activity around the circle.
- Watching how other pupils do it.
- Waiting.
- Anticipating their turn.
- Passing the activity to their neighbour.

Circle activities using physical movement
Pupils learn to develop their skills of permission, choice, assertion, negotiation, by structured interaction within the circle, involving e.g. walking, throwing or rolling items across to other members of the group.

Matching
Within the circle, or a small group, pupils are asked in turn to match items e.g. objects with pictures of places or objects with pictures of people. This can achieve several different aims:

- to differentiate people of different age groups;
- to understand where objects belong;
- to become familiar with new or unknown objects;
- to understand the difference between public and private.

Experiential work
Pupils learn some things by experiencing them in the classroom. They can be asked to feel, to taste, to smell, to listen, and to identify, discriminate or state their preferences. They can be given a sense of what being 'private' means, by setting up a separate area of the room, for instance. And they can experience being a member of a group, by experiencing the impact of their own behaviour on the group, and vice versa.

Using imagination/mime
Pupils watch or engage in a situation they may never have encountered. They can practise their skills in situations with which they are familiar. They can be helped to discriminate between what is 'real' and what is 'fantasy'.

Distancing techniques
These are ways of enabling pupils to discuss sensitive or personal issues without personal disclosure (see p. 38).

Putting it all together

What does all this mean in practice? Once we have assessed pupils' needs and decided on a theme, appropriate activities can be chosen from these categories. The following examples are developed from the Health Education in Scottish Schools guidance (Eales and Watson 1994) and *Let's Do It* (Johns *et al.* 1997).

- Group building

  - Passing the hat (the cushion, the balloon) as you say your name.
  - Make a shape as you say your name and then other pupils say their name.
  - My name is . . . and I like . . .
  - Change your seats if . . . using a simple category, e.g. all those with short hair.

- Public and private

  - Making a PRIVATE sign to put on the door.
  - Matching pictures of public and private activities with places.
  - No, that's private (like 'Simon says').

- Gender

  - All change (e.g. if you are a woman).
  - Voices on tape: which gender?
  - The clothes game: identifying clothing as for males or females.

- Body parts

  - Passing the cushion with body parts.
  - Large body outline and body 'bits' to place on the outline.
  - The clothes game, e.g. what does a bra/boxer shorts cover?

- Body function

  - Identifying body fluids: making fake fluids and matching them to parts of the body.
  - Story telling and picture stories, e.g. menstruation and masturbation stories.
  - Matching toiletries with parts of the body, on body outlines or other pictures.
  - The chemist's shop: buying appropriate toiletries for different body functions, e.g. sanitary towels

- Life cycle

  - Matching pictures of objects with photographs of people of different ages.
  - Body changes, using pictures of people growing up.

- Feelings

  - What is the feeling? Using a range of pictures.
  - What's in the box? Guess the feeling.
  - Assertion/permission/saying no.
  - Do you like this? (response yes/no).
  - Can I shake your hand?
  - Can I look in your bag?

- Relationships

  - The phone game: an imaginary conversation – who is at the other end?
  - Guess the role: café scene with two people meeting. Are they friends or strangers?
  - Matching relationships, using a collection of photographs, e.g. Who fancies who?
  - Story telling, using models or pictures.
  - Case studies and scenarios.

- Safer sex

  - Musical condoms – played like 'Pass the Parcel'. Each time the music stops, the package is undone a little more; this reduces the embarrassment when the condom is finally revealed.
  - How strong is a condom? Using water to fill them.

These activities are described in detail in *Let's Do It*, published by Image in Action; and in *Talking Together about Growing Up*, published by the FPA.

Programme planning

Three examples of programme planning follow. The first and second describe an outline SRE curriculum for primary and secondary age pupils, originally planned for pupils with severe learning disabilities. These could easily be adapted for pupils with different abilities. The third shows how gender as a theme can be organised across the curriculum.

A curriculum plan for primary pupils with severe learning disabilities

Key Stage 1   Reception–Year Three

Learning to be in a group:

- working in a circle;
- saying their name and the name of others;
- taking turns;
- developing basic social skills, e.g. eye contact.

Themes

- Body parts: recognition and naming of body parts, e.g. hands, feet, (using different methods such as songs and painting).
- Gender, e.g. identifying as a male or female.
- Public and private: understanding the difference between public and private parts of the body and public and private places.

- Feelings: naming them and acknowledging them as well as being valued by staff and other pupils.
- Relationships: recognition that there is self and there are others; recognising differences, e.g. hair colour.
- Life cycle: recognising family relationships, and that these are different from relationships at school.

Key Stage 2   Years Four–Five

This requires the development of group safety through circle activities including trust games and taking turns. They should be beginning to develop the skills of

- assertion;
- giving permission;
- making decisions.

Themes

- Body parts – naming all body parts including the sexual parts.
- Gender – boy/girl, man/woman. Recognition of their gender and the gender of others.
- Public and private – where is a private place at home?
- Feelings – recognising and naming own feelings, and recognising that they can have an effect on others.
- Relationships – appropriate touch, developing friendships and co-operation in groups.
- Life cycle: difference between themselves as children and as babies.

Year Six

- Group identity and ownership – understanding that it is their space and they can determine the working agreement that clarifies the ways they will work together.
- Understanding that the session is private.
- Making choices about activities and leading some activities.
- Developing assertiveness work – understanding the implications of saying yes and no and developing the skills to make real choices in and out of school.

Themes

- Body parts – naming public and private body parts and understanding body functions such as menstruation.
- Gender – identifying the physical differences between boys and girls, men and women.
- Public and private – identifying private places and gender distinctions relating to privacy.
- Feelings – clarifying the feelings that they have and that others may have and building up their feelings 'vocabulary'.

- Relationships – identifying the range of relationships in and outside school including family, friends, strangers.
- Life cycle – identifying the life cycle and understanding the process i.e. baby, child, teenager, adult. This will include body changes and puberty.

A curriculum plan for secondary pupils with severe learning disabilities

Themes from the primary years are reinforced and developed in the secondary phase. Often this means repeating earlier work to provide a basis for the more explicit work in the later years.

Key Stage 3   Years Seven–Nine

Activities will be used to develop the group especially if this is a new group. This will include working in a circle and taking turns. The themes in Year 6 will be reinforced and extended.

Themes

- Body parts – naming public and private body parts and understanding body functions including menstruation and masturbation.
- Gender – understanding the physical differences between men and women.
- Public and private – understanding the privacy required for masturbation and developing their understanding of their rights to privacy.
- Feelings – understanding the changes in and consequences of feelings, including sexual feelings.
- Relationships – understanding the importance of their peer group and how they relate to one another. Developing strategies for forming friendships
- Life cycle – understanding body changes as they grow and change.

Key Stage 4   Years Ten and Eleven

Continue the reinforcement of group identity with an emphasis on making decisions and practising assertion and negotiation skills within the group and helping pupils to transfer their knowledge to situations outside the school. At this stage it is important to offer more opportunities for independent choices and action. Work should also develop on sexual relationships and feelings.

Themes

- Body parts – understanding the sexual body parts and similarities and differences between the sexes. Understanding the range of physical abilities and disabilities and awareness of race, culture and faith.
- Gender – exploring and recognising stereotypes.
- Public and private – offering opportunities to create a private space and

transferring the concept to other situations including developing a sense of privacy such as in the bathroom and bedroom. Understanding appropriate sexual and emotional behaviour.

- Feelings – recognising physiological response and developing a language for them. Managing responses to feelings including sexual feelings and arousal.
- Relationships – developing skills for friendships and the development of sexual relationships and understanding safer sex and contraception.
- Life cycle – understanding sexual body changes and changing relationships with friends and families.

Older pupils 16–19

Much of the material covered will repeat and reinforce earlier learning, but this is where the particular needs and abilities of the pupils will influence choice and development of topics.

Themes

- Body parts – including the sexual function of body parts. Developing an understanding of support available for sexual activity if physical disability makes it difficult.
- Gender – exploring and challenging gender and racial stereotypes and different roles in parenting.
- Public and private – understanding their own and other people's need for privacy including privacy for an intimate relationship. Developing an understanding of confidentiality.
- Feelings – understanding sexual feelings, sexual desire and sexual response and an awareness of their own and others' sexual feelings.
- Relationships – skills for developing an intimate relationship. Developing an awareness of the range of sexual relationships including same sex relationships. Developing their understanding of sexual health, safer sex and HIV.
- Life cycle – learning about the use of contraception, understanding conception, pregnancy and birth including parenting and child rearing. Learning about sources of support.

Curriculum theme: gender, 2–19 years

This demonstrates how gender can be developed as a theme throughout the curriculum.

Nursery 2–5 years

- Toilet training
- Stereotypical gender roles
- Student groupings
- Language (boy, girl)

Infant 5–8 years

- To identify gender of others
- To identify gender differences (I am a girl; he is a boy)
- Use of gender-specific language (he, she, mum, dad, boy, girl)
- Gender in a social context (toilet labels, changing rooms).

Junior 8–11 years

- To identify the gender of others
- To identify gender roles, e.g. shaving, make-up
- To identify gender relations, e.g. sister, mother, daughter; brother, uncle
- Privacy related to undressing, e.g. swimming
- School/public labels, e.g. toilets, changing rooms
- Gender-related religious observance, places of worship.

Senior 11–19 years

- To be aware of the social context of (gender-related) behaviour
- To develop concepts of masculine/feminine
- To be aware of secondary sexual characteristics
- To learn about relationships
- Body parts: sexual body changes
- Public/private body parts, and behaviour
- Masculine/feminine appearance, clothes, etc.
- Changing interests and emotions
- Cultural and religious rites of passage (bar mitzvah, confirmation, weddings)
- Cultural gender roles and expectations
- Sexual body functions (menstruation, wet dreams)
- Community visits or visitors, e.g. to a chemist's shop or a sexual health service.

Additional work for 16–19s

- Changing sexual feelings
- Expectations of role: the future
- Sexual relationships and sexual orientation
- Masturbation
- Contraception
- Introducing the idea of adult 'objects' and adult behaviour e.g. make-up, alcohol, clothes preferences, sexual image, condoms
- Community visits or visitors, e.g. sexual health service.

Working with different abilities

Whatever the abilities or disabilities of pupils, the principles remain the same. There may be differences of emphasis, but the active methodology can be used with success. Certainly, there may be limits for the level of work that is possible with pupils with multiple and complex needs, although some of the foundation and basic stages have been used with those pupils. And the methods have been shown to work with more able pupils with moderate learning disabilities: in a trial project with 16–19 year olds, it was reported 'the methods appear to be effective for practising skills and enabling members to test out new ways of behaving in a safe environment'.

Figure 7.1 shows how well various methods work with groups of different abilities. Methods that are particularly successful with pupils with moderate learning disabilities are role play, drama games, case study material, and video.

	Severe Learning Disabilities	Moderate Learning Disabilities
Working agreements	*	*
Brainstorming	X	*
Case studies	X	*
Discussion	X	X
Matching (e.g. photos with activities)	*	*
Circle work	*	*
Games	*	*
Drama games	*	*
Music activities	*	*
3-D models	*	*
Penis model	*	*
Body outlines work	*	*
Body function activities	*	*
Role play	*	*
Developing characters for role play	Less so	*
Video	X	*
Single sex groups at times	*	*

Note: * - Suitable for use with this group of children and young people.
X - Unsuitable for use with this group of children and young people.

Figure 7.1 Effectiveness of methods with different ability groups

The methods can be used at a different pace, activities can be used once or many times and materials used will be different. However, what we have found is that there is a central compendium of successful methods that can work effectively with pupils of a very wide range of abilities, albeit adapted and paced differently. Many of these activities work well with mainstream groups too, which is encouraging for those of us who work with children and young people with special needs who are now educated in mainstream schools.

However, even more careful planning is needed to make sure that the less able pupils are fully included. Similar methods have been used effectively with children and young people with physical disabilities, even though many of them have no learning disability.

Schools are in a key position, in partnership with parents and carers, to support children and young people, through puberty and adolescence, with a positive, well-structured programme of sex and relationships education. This, coupled with extra-curricular activities, will go some way to ensuring that children and young people with disabilities develop positive relationships and are able to recognise and resist harm and abuse and develop positive levels of self-esteem.

8 Sex and relationships education in Pupil Referral Units

Pupils attending Pupil Referral Units (PRUs) have been excluded from their mainstream schools, are at risk of exclusion for presenting challenging behaviour or are school refusers. They generally attend on a part-time basis although there is some full-time provision for Key Stage 4 pupils. The principles of effective practice outlined in Chapter 3 apply within this setting and the same learning outcomes outlined in Chapters 5 and 6 should be worked towards depending on the age of the pupil. Effective partnerships will need to be developed with the school if pupils are dual registered to ensure that they receive their entitlement to SRE.

This chapter identifies some of the particular challenges of working in a PRU. It is based on a national survey of SRE provision in PRUs carried out by the Sex Education Forum followed by more intensive work with pupils and staff in PRUs in East Sussex, Brighton and Hove. It also contains a case study of a SRE programme developed in Francis Barber PRU in Tooting, south-west London.

Pupil Referral Units

With an increasing emphasis on inclusion in mainstream settings, how education is provided for children and young people excluded from school is under constant change and review. Many PRUs will be across split sites, some will be attached to a school as a behaviour unit and some LEAs aim to completely reintegrate excluded pupils. This chapter addresses additional issues for working with this group of children and young people and should be read in conjunction with Chapter 3.

Children and young people in PRUs

Children as young as seven are temporarily or permanently excluded from school and spend time in PRUs. Children and young people attending a Pupil Referral Unit are more likely to experience poor emotional and sexual health. They are more likely to experience early pregnancy (Social Exclusion Unit 1999). A higher than average proportion are likely to have been abused or hurt. Many pupils in PRUs will have been told that they are failures and/or written themselves off and internalised feelings of low self-esteem. There are examples of excellent practice where teachers and their partners ensure that these children and young people receive positive SRE that supports their emotional development and self-esteem. Respondents to the survey emphasised that the social and health inequalities that these children and young people experience make it important that those advisory and support teams who provide support, such as healthy schools co-ordinators and LEA Advisers, pay particular attention to the needs of both staff and pupils in PRUs.

It is often assumed that pupils in PRUs (particularly older pupils) are sexually active and knowledgeable (Blake *et al.* 2001). This is often not the case and SRE is vital in supporting pupils in developing knowledge and emotional and social skills. Pupils who are excluded from school are likely to have experienced negative relationships and may find it difficult to interact effectively. This might be a response to authority and/or each other or to a wider set of circumstances. Although formal SRE is likely to be building on a foundation of negative experience, it can form part of a planned programme of opportunities to build self-esteem and help pupils map a different future in terms of their own relationships.

The environment in PRUs and the whole-setting ethos

A positive environment can be provided for all children and young people attending PRUs. Practitioners emphasised the importance of considering the physical surroundings. Many PRUs are in poor accommodation and this can add to the sense of failure and low self-esteem amongst pupils. Effort is spent on creating a positive environment that will aid learning. Children and young people have often been involved in decorating or making posters that can help create a positive learning environment.

Some questions workers in PRUs have asked include:

- Is it welcoming?
- Does it include work that has been done by the pupils?
- Is it suitable for their age and stage of development?

The whole-setting ethos needs to feel safe for all of its pupils. Many pupils in PRUs display sexist, racist and homophobic attitudes. One young women stated how it can feel unsafe in a PRU as she is in a minority. She described sexual bullying and harassment. This type of behaviour needs to be addressed. All staff can work together to agree ways of challenging appropriately so that there are consistent messages in both the formal and informal curriculum, at the same time ensuring that it feels safe for the challenged as well.

Key skills

*All I can hope for is having enough skills to be able to get a job and to mix
with other people. (young man, aged 13)*

Colleagues working in PRUs confirmed that the primary aim of work with these pupils is to support their personal and social development and help develop key skills. Many PRUs work within a key skills curriculum for all of their subject work. Key skills operate at a number of levels and are important as they help pupils to focus on what they are learning and how they are learning so they can achieve more, be flexible in their future employment and organise their personal lives and overcome problems. The Qualifications and Curriculum Authority outlines six key skills. These are:

- communication including speaking, listening, reading and writing;
- application of number which is about interpreting information to do with numbers, doing calculations and presenting your findings;
- information technology which includes being able to use a computer to find, develop and present information including text, numbers and images;
- working with others which includes working in a pair or small group and taking leadership;
- improving your own learning and performance;
- problem solving.

SRE can be developed to support specific learning about sex, relationships and sexual health while paying attention to the particular key skills. For further information about key skills, visit the Qualifications and Curriculum Authority website www.qca.org.uk.

The national Award Scheme Development Accreditation Network (ASDAN) has worked with the Sex Education Forum and the National Children's Bureau to develop a sex and relationships education module that supports the development of key skills (Blake 2001). This has been used successfully in PRUs across the country. The module contributes to national accreditation that can significantly contribute to raising PRU pupils' self-esteem and desire for learning.

The organisation of PSHE and Citizenship

The survey showed that PSHE and Citizenship is best developed when there is a PSHE and Citizenship co-ordinator who is able to lead the development of effective SRE by doing the following:

- developing, reviewing and monitoring policy and practice;
- contacting schools where pupils are dual registered to identify what SRE they will receive in their mainstream setting;
- supporting staff in planning and delivery, including identifying professional development opportunities;
- identifying appropriate resources including outside visitors.

Some PRUs have found it helpful to have a specialist PSHE and Citizenship teacher who is responsible for delivering PSHE and Citizenship to all year groups as it builds confidence and group cohesion.

Policy development and planning

There are a number of issues that are specific to PRUs and these can helpfully be addressed in the policy. These are additional to those discussed in Chapter 3 that are relevant across all settings. Effective policies support worker confidence by addressing issues such as confidentiality, harassment and bullying. They also clarify how PRUs will link with relevant schools and other sources of help and support such as Connexions personal advisers.

It is established best practice to engage with parents in the development of policy. Although many PRUs find it difficult to engage parents in all aspects of their children's education, Francis Barber PRU has used their review meetings with parents at the end of term. They used a questionnaire to survey the views of parents at this meeting and this enabled the PSHE and Citizenship co-ordinator to feel confident of parental support and to encourage parents to reinforce the learning in the home.

PSHE and Citizenship, like all other subjects, is best co-ordinated for pupils who are dual registered or on short-term placements in the PRU. Co-ordinators have secured pupil interest in the topic by ensuring a core entitlement for SRE that meets the individual needs of pupils and does not laboriously repeat previous learning. If pupils are attending two educational establishments, colleagues in PRUs emphasise the importance of ensuring that information about provision in the mainstream setting is obtained and that they feed back the work that they have been doing to schools and parents.

Without this dialogue it is likely that issues will be missed or repeated. In the consultations with pupils in PRUs, one of their frequent complaints was that the material had been previously covered elsewhere and it was 'boring'.

Curriculum planning

As with all SRE, pupils' views should be sought during the planning of SRE. These children and young people are less likely than others to have been asked their opinions and may require extra support to do so. Many of the children and young people in PRUs will have lower than average literacy levels and consultations are usefully done through structured oral consultation or using draw and write activities. Where consultation does take place, like all pupils they have great ideas as to how to improve SRE. One PRU carried out consultation with pupils who stated that they wanted to use computers. This was built into the SRE programme and pupils reported enjoying the lessons and assessment showed that they learnt about sex and relationships as well as developing the key skill of ICT.

PRUs should have an up-to-date scheme of work that clearly identifies learning outcomes and a core curriculum for part-time pupils. These should be in line with the learning outcomes suggested by Ofsted (2002). Many pupils will be poor or infrequent attendees of the PRU and planning takes account of this in terms of the exercises that are used.

When planning SRE, remember that many pupils have difficulty forming positive relationships or working in groups and therefore tasks need to be set that they will be able to achieve. This may mean working individually or in friendship pairs, providing extra support in the classroom to help with the task or ensuring that the activities are structured in a way that enables them to work confidently with peers. If pupils start quarrelling or acting up, they may well have done so in Maths; it is not necessarily the SRE content. Attention needs to be paid to the group process, the needs of the individual and the content.

Pupils in PRUs tend to have lower than average emotional and academic literacy levels. Effective planning takes account of shorter attention spans. Activities that enable movement and 'quick wins' such as the completion of a quiz or hard outcomes such as posters that can be displayed secure commitment and interest.

Teacher relationships, role modelling and making it safe

Teachers in the survey identified that staff in PRUs often build close relationships with pupils. This is positive but they found it equally important to maintain the boundaries between education and personal information about sex and relationships. One young man described feeling as though he knew the teacher too well to talk about sex and relationships with her. To feel safe he needed to be sure that they were not going to talk about him with the staff team. When talking with him, however, it was clear that he did not always maintain this boundary himself and would often talk about personal experiences. This can be addressed by developing working agreements and being clear and explicit about the expectations in SRE. Teachers ensure that pupils do not talk about their own personal experiences in the classroom as it is a public place.

Pupils reported the importance of knowing about the range of individuals and agencies that can offer specific help and support for personal issues, thus reinforcing the distinction between education and pastoral support.

Using outside agencies

Where visitors participate in the taught SRE programme, colleagues emphasised the importance of being well prepared and briefed. Visitors need to be aware of and agree to work within the values framework of the PRU, and must be clear about boundaries, confidentiality and their roles and responsibilities. Where they are not used to working with disengaged children and young people, colleagues have found it useful to offer the following advice to visitors:

- Use short activities and shorter time planned for discussions.
- Offer clear and concrete, specific tasks that everyone can achieve.
- Celebrate success and offer really positive praise and feedback.

It is useful if somebody who is trusted by the pupils introduces visitors to the group. This will probably be a worker within the PRU. This reduces fear, mistrust and hostility towards the visitor. Often one-off sessions are not helpful for this group because it takes longer to build an effective working relationship and therefore longer timescales need to be planned.

Good practice in the classroom

Developing a working agreement

Many PRUs have a behaviour contract, or a home/school agreement. PRUs have built on this to develop a specific working agreement for SRE. It is important not to offer an unrealistic confidentiality agreement, but instead to remind pupils that the classroom is a public place and therefore confidentiality cannot be maintained. This helps create a safe learning environment.

Developing rituals

Many pupils, particularly those who are more vulnerable, will not be confident with new topic areas. SRE needs to match the maturity level of the pupils as well as using a range of teaching methodologies to keep pupils engaged in the learning process. Developing rituals within SRE can help pupils to develop confidence in the process.

Planning activities

Activities need to be short, clear and specific. So, for example, instead of having an open-ended discussion, pupils may be asked to answer one or two very specific questions. Feedback to the whole group should be kept to a minimum so there is less likelihood of becoming bored. As with all groups of children and young people, activities need to be designed so that all can achieve at their own level and can experience success.

Staff initiating or supervising discussion groups should be well prepared to respond to any issues that may arise from the discussion either with the group/class or with an individual after the session.

While all sessions are planned with clear learning objectives, the SRE programme needs to be sufficiently flexible to respond to immediate issues raised by pupils. If a topic is causing interest or concern, then it is helpful to stick with that issue and maximise the moment as a positive experience of learning. If this means that the planned objectives are not met, this can be recorded and revisited either by you or by a colleague at a later date. This applies to outside visitors as well as staff members.

Some issues will be difficult, too personal or inappropriate for the classroom. Where this is true, it needs to be followed up by a staff member and pupils can be referred to the local community services.

Celebrating success

Pupils in PRUs are unlikely to have been achievers in many aspects of education. Central to their engagement is making SRE interesting and manageable, offering positive affirmation and celebrating success. Displaying work that has been carried out by pupils provides a clear message that their work is valued and valuable. Wherever possible, pupils should receive accreditation for their work through key skills and any other accredited programme they are involved in.

SRE for a Year 11 boys' group

Francis Barber Pupil Referral Unit is situated in the London Borough of Wandsworth. It is the only Pupil Referral Unit in the Borough, responding to the referrals of all secondary-aged pupils. The PRU provides a service for those pupils who are out of school, or who are experiencing difficulties in school. Well over 50 per cent of pupils referred to Francis Barber are permanently excluded, with the remainder being either non-attenders or dual registered. There is increasing pressure on the PRU to work with dual registered young people.

The PRU community is a diverse one with multiple needs. The staff at the Unit aim to provide a positive experience of academic and social learning in a safe and supportive environment, where individuals feel accepted. Great care is taken to maintain a pleasant physical environment as well as establishing positive relationships through a continuous emphasis on 'key working'. Each pupil has a named key worker responsible for his or her well-being. The key worker is the main point of contact and source of support for the young person.

SRE is considered of vital importance to the pupils since the majority of them experience difficulties in forming positive relationships or have experienced dysfunctional/abusive relationships. Exclusion/'failure' at school diminishes self-esteem and pupils frequently have barriers to learning of both an emotional and academic nature – from low literacy to high levels of anger. There is a strong emphasis on positive relationships within the classroom and around the Unit. If positive relationships and an emphasis on emotional literacy are sought, self-esteem improves and learning is made easier.

At Francis Barber SRE is delivered by the PSHE co-ordinator, with another professional. This has traditionally been a Young Persons Health Adviser. Pupils are taught in mixed groups of up to seven pupils, with some single gender sessions – two-thirds of the roll are boys. Here Lorraine King, PSHE Coordinator, describes the learning from her Unit.

First and foremost, a SRE programme begins with the needs and priorities of the pupils in the group. Sessions are planned using the frameworks for PSHE and Citizenship as a guide, with a focus on the four strands. Therefore SRE is placed in context. At Francis Barber, the work begins with establishing positive relationships through a strong values framework. The teenage pregnancy worker and PSHE co-ordinator ran a six-week project for Year 11 boys followed by a project aimed at Year 11 girls. This case study focuses on the boys' group and the outcomes of the work.

Aims of the programme:

- raise the self-esteem of young people;
- increase confidence to access advice and information about health issues (particularly sexual and emotional health) within the community;
- give young people the opportunity to make informed choices which promote their own and other people's health;
- identify and meet the needs of both genders in an attempt to improve emotional literacy;
- promote understanding of risk-taking situations and enhance pupils' abilities to deal with these positively.

Each session was tightly planned with specific aims all linked to the development of key skills. Sessions were conducted in a circle throughout with food provided at the end of the session in an attempt to create a further sense of group identity. Sessions were as follows:

- Introduction to the project – overall aims, working agreement, concept of 'relationship', questionnaire on self-esteem.
- Positive choices – describing positive/negative experiences and associated feelings, preparation for a visitor.
- Visitor – a dad – focus on parenting/relationships.
- Dealing with conflict – visitor discussing anger management.
- Social activity – preparing a meal and inviting chosen adults.
- Sexual language – parts of the male and female body.
- Sexual language – the use of insults and aggression.
- Pupil questions and answers.
- Discussing feelings – a 'feelings wheel' on which words describing different emotions were displayed to facilitate expression.
- Visitor – Health Adviser.

The project was initially intended to last for six sessions but was extended because the group members were enjoying the classes so much.

From this work we learnt the following:

- SRE in single gender groups worked well and some single gender teaching is essential (if possible), since specific issues may be explored in greater depth (we invited a father to discuss his experiences as a dad, for example).
- Young men do talk and welcome the opportunity to discuss sex and relationships issues.
- SRE is best delivered in an environment encouraging positive relationships The boys felt relaxed with me (as their key worker and PSHE teacher) and the teenage pregnancy worker (new to them but accepted due to a gentle and calm approach and being introduced and working with a trusted figure).
- The quality of the relationships was already established prior to this work (a values framework with PSHE at its core), and there was no need for bravado.
- It is important to have a private space for the sessions without interruption. This reinforces the sense of a safe and secure environment (other staff were made aware of the sessions and privacy was respected).
- Working agreements were established by the group at the start of the project and were used to check conduct and maintain respectful behaviour towards each other.
- The use of positive role models was invaluable for initiating relevant discussions. There were two visitors – one spoke on fatherhood and the other on anger management. It was useful to have a man speaking about his feelings and role as a dad since this made the boys reflect on their own fathers and their relationships with them, as well as the realities of fatherhood. The second visitor was organised in response to a request made by one of the pupils, following an earlier session. The group appreciated someone visiting and speaking to them openly.

- As with all work in PRUs, there needs to be flexibility to react to current situations. Often sessions were altered because a young person expressed an interest in discussing an issue further – anger, for example.
- Sessions need to be of reasonable length, especially if visitors are to be included. We found that sessions of 40 minutes were too short and our sessions tended to extend to 50/55 minutes, which included the preparation and consumption of food.
- Team teaching provided additional support for both pupils and adults. It is helpful if one of the adults is a specialist in a particular area – pregnancy/drugs/sexual health.

9 Professional development

I think that it would be helpful to actually have a bit of support for the teachers, because it is, like, quite unfair to expect them to be able to teach about sex because that is not what they are trained to do. (young woman, aged 15)

Effective teachers feel confident both with the content and the process of active learning. This has been recognised at a national level and there is a pilot scheme currently being run by the Department for Education and Skills to accredit the teaching of PSHE. This accreditation process sits within the broader teachers' continuing professional development strategy. For further information contact Roz Caught, National Healthy School Standard, the Health Development Agency (see Useful organisations).

There is a broad range of ways to develop professional competence. Although traditionally much professional development took place outside of the classroom, there is an increasing trend towards classroom-based development such as team teaching, self-reflection and assessment through the collection of evidence. The type of development opportunity you require will depend on the learning need. Taking time to clearly define your need will be helpful in ensuring that the need is best met by the method. With increasingly limited opportunities for off-site opportunities, knowing what you want to achieve is important before setting out to find a training course that will satisfy it.

There are a number of national and local agencies that offer training and support in sex and relationships education (see Useful organisations). This chapter aims to provide some opportunities for self-reflection and self review. It is not intended to replace formal training, but instead to support you in self-assessment, self-reflection, and where relevant, help you to identify further learning needs. Going through this process could help in the setting of your personal development objectives. The exercises can be adapted for use within a staff team.

Self-assessment

This self-assessment sheet provides a baseline analysis of your current level of skills, confidence and competence. You could put a date on the sheet so that you can revisit it and make a comparison.

	1. Not very confident 2. Quite confident 3. Confident 4. Very confident	Comments
How well do you know and understand the policy and values framework in your setting? (see p. 18)		
How confident are you in planning clear aims and objectives and choosing suitable activities? (see p. 22)		
How confident are you in using a range of different active learning methods? (see pp. 40–2, 84–7)		
How confident are you in meeting and responding to the differing needs of pupils in your class? (see pp. 55–60)		
How confident are you in monitoring and assessing pupil learning in SRE? (see pp. 50–4)		
How confident are you in working with outside agencies? (see p. 25–8)		
How confident are you in referring young people to community health and advisory services? (see pp. 79–80)		

Language

The language we use can:

- Convey our level of comfort with a topic. Often we rely on overly formal terms, give 'family names' or use euphemisms if we are uncomfortable with a topic.
- Explicitly or implicitly exclude groups of people. Using terms like husband and wife can infer that you are not talking about people who are not married or who are not heterosexual. Other words such as 'foreplay' may suggest that all people have penetrative sex, which is not true.
- Reinforce prejudice and discrimination. Slang terms are often derogatory and the meaning may not be realised. For example, children may use the term gay without fully understanding the meaning; however, the learning is that gay is bad or wrong.
- Be used as a way of trying to maintain authority or gain credibility. Language can be used to maintain authority, for example, by not allowing children and young people to use language that they feel comfortable with such as 'willy' or can be used to gain credibility such as use of street terms for sexual behaviour or parts. Young people generally do not want adults to try and appear cool by adopting 'their' language. However, they do not want to feel inhibited from using language they feel comfortable with. This is a sensitive balance and it is important that you do not encourage prejudice or be seen to be colluding with it.

Some school policies will explicitly refer to language that can be used in the classrooms. You need to be familiar with your school's agreed policy.

Exercise 1

1. Think about the following words and phrases and when you might use them in the classroom.
2. Note in the second column the context in which you might currently use these terms.
3. In the third column think about the messages that you might be sending when you use this word.
4. In the fourth column think about a word or phrase that you might use in the future to ensure inclusivity.

Word used	Where you might currently use the word	What messages might you be inferring when using this word or term?	An alternative word or phrase that you might use in the future
Boyfriend			
Girlfriend			
Husband			
Wife			
Partner			
Normal			
Sex			
Gay sex			
Foreplay			
Straight sex			
Oral sex			
Anal sex			
Vaginal sex			
Parents			
Mum and Dad			
Carers			

Self-reflection

- Which ones are suitable for you to use in the classroom in all contexts?
- Which ones are not suitable for you to use in the classroom in all contexts?
- Which ones are inclusive of people with different home backgrounds, sexualities and life-styles?
- Which ones exclude people implicitly or explicitly?
- What will you change in your classroom practice?

Exercise 2

Think about and list all the different names including slang names for:

- sexual activity
- female sexual parts
- male sexual parts

Sexual activity	Female sexual parts	Male sexual parts

Self-reflection

- Which ones do young people use?
- Which ones are you comfortable using?
- How will you negotiate and agree language with pupils?
- Which ones are suitable for you to use in the classroom and fit in with your school policy?
- Which ones are not suitable for you to use in the classroom in all contexts?
- Which ones are inclusive of people with different home backgrounds, sexualities and life styles?
- Which ones exclude people implicitly or explicitly?
- What will you change in your classroom practice?

The scope of SRE

The quotes below are from children and young people involved in a number of consultation events carried out by the Sex Education Forum and the National Children's Bureau. They reflect some areas that children, young people and research tell us are generally not covered well in SRE. Think about the following quotes and consider whether you agree or disagree with them. Note down your responses to aid self-reflection.

If you are a PSHE co-ordinator you could do this with the teachers who deliver SRE by reading them out one at a time and discussing them before considering the self-review questions.

1. We need to practise saying yes and no, really making sure we can make decisions.
2. All we ever get told is about the bad things that can happen like pregnancy and diseases. There must be some good bits, otherwise why would people do it? We need to learn about those bits too.
3. They should teach you about the gay issues as well.
4. How boys and girls are expected to behave is an important part of it.
5. Prejudice is based on ignorance and we need to be taught about it so we do not have ignorance in our society.
6. We need to learn about feelings, relationships, that sort of thing.
7. It needs to take account of different religious and cultural beliefs.
8. We need to think about real-life situations, like what leads on to sex.
9. We need to know where we can go to get information and advice about contraception.
10. They keep saying, 'Save yourself, wait until you are married.' It just is not realistic in this country. Maybe in other countries, but not here, no, no way.
11. Sometimes people get drunk, it's all a bit messy and its not easy to know what to do. We need to think about these types of things.
12. They leave it too late – we need to start learning about puberty and sex in primary school.
13. Boys mess around and make it difficult to ask questions.
14. Just because I have a disability it does not mean that I won't have relationships. Sometimes, it feels like everyone expects me to stay in forever.
15. Nobody ever talks about sex, what it is actually like.

Self-reflection

- What are you already doing well?
- Are there any areas that you are not covering already?
- What areas of the curriculum need further development?
- What do you need to do as part of this curriculum development?
- What are the policy and practice review needs?
- What are the professional development needs?

Confidentiality

The boundaries of confidentiality should be clearly laid out in your school confidentiality policy that will cover all aspects of school life. Being familiar with the policy is important. Confidentiality policies should be focused on the needs of children and young people.

The following three scenarios are real-life situations that can be used to stimulate reflection and or discussion in the development or review of your policy. The law and best practice for each scenario are outlined on pp. 114–15.

Nadine

You are the form teacher of Nadine who is 15. She tells you that she is pregnant and needs to see a doctor. She does not want to tell her parents and she wants an abortion.

Points to consider
- What does your school policy say you should do in this situation?
- How will you establish what Nadine needs and wants you to do?
- If you have to tell the head teacher or member of the senior management team, have you discussed this with Nadine before doing it?
- Have you talked to Nadine about telling her parents and offered her support to do this?
- Has Nadine got support from her friends or partner?
- If you are going to take her to the clinic, are you insured to do so?
- If your confidentiality policy is not best practice, what steps will you take to get support for the policy to be reviewed?

Asaf

At the end of a sex education lesson 15-year-old Asaf comes up to you and tells you that he is gay and he is having a relationship with another young man in the school.

Points to consider
- What does your school policy say you should do in this situation?
- How will you establish what Asaf needs and wants you to do?
- Do you need to review current SRE to ensure it meets the needs of gay and lesbian pupils?
- Are there community youth groups or services for gay and lesbian pupils that Asaf should know about?

Tasha

Tasha has HIV. You are her head of year and are aware of her HIV status. A discussion in PSHE about HIV is tense and difficult with lots of prejudice being demonstrated. She is visibly distressed but has not left the classroom.

Points to consider

- How will you challenge the prejudice in a way that is safe for Tasha and safe for the young people demonstrating prejudice?
- Do you need to talk to Tasha after the class has finished?
- Is it appropriate to discuss the incident with her form tutor, parent or carer?
- What further work does the school need to do on HIV and prejudice? Is HIV explicitly addressed in the equal opportunities policy?

Facilitation skills

There is a range of skills that teachers can use to ensure effective learning. These are described in Chapter 3. The following extracts are based on real-life sex and relationships education sessions. The teacher's responses and interventions have been taken out. Where there is an empty box, think about the type of response or intervention that you might make to maintain safety, clarify the issues and ensure learning.

Primary school

Mixed sex group, 8-year-old children.

	Jamie said he saw something like that on the television.
	He saw people kissing and sexing each other.
Think of an open question	
	Raz said that he was going to sex me.
	Uhh, that is rude.
	What is sex? (Lots of giggling).
How you would answer this question?	

After the lesson has finished, it is playtime. At the end of playtime Jack comes to you and says, 'Matthew says you've got babies in your balls. You haven't, have you?'

| How would you reply? |
| |

Secondary school

Mixed sex group, 14-year-old young people. They are feeding back their thoughts from small group discussions. They were given the following case study to discuss:

Paul and Rosie have been going out together for a few months. Rosie wants to have sex but Paul does not.

They were asked to consider the following questions:

What might Paul be feeling?

What might Paul be thinking?

What might Paul do?

What might Rosie be feeling?

What might Rosie be thinking?

What might Rosie do?

The whole group are discussing their ideas. Below are some extracts.

	Rosie might be feeling as though maybe Paul does not fancy her.
	She might be wondering what is wrong with her.
	Paul should explain that he does not feel ready and she should accept that and not hassle him.
	Yeah, but why doesn't he want to have sex with her? It is a bit weird.
How might you respond to this?	
	I think he might be feeling annoyed that she is pressuring him.
	He definitely should not have sex with her if he is not ready to.
	They need to talk about it and sort it out.

	What if they can't sort it out though?
	Maybe they can't carry on going out with each other.
	But that is stupid just because he doesn't feel ready for sex they are going to finish.
How might you summarise their ideas?	
You want to get them to think about effective communication in relationships. Think of an open question.	

A classroom discussion has led into discussion about gender roles and expectations. You have asked them why there are different 'rules' for young men and young women about sex and relationships.

	Girls should be able to do what they like without people calling them slags.
	White girls are slags. They just sleep around.
	So are some boys but that is supposed to be cool.
	Boys need sex more than girls anyway.
How would you summarise the different views? What are the key messages to reaffirm?	

Best practice advice for confidentiality case studies

Nadine

Best practice is having a policy that supports you in helping Nadine to access help from a health professional while encouraging her to involve her parents. Generally parents do not respond as negatively as their sons and daughters expect. However, it is important to respect Nadine's request not to tell her parents. In almost all cases the young woman will tell her parents and, after some initial distress, parents do support their child.

In a few cases parents may be hostile and unsupportive. In other cases the pregnancy may be the result of sexual abuse in the family. Offering positive support to Nadine will enable the teacher to understand the situation more and offer appropriate support to tell her parents or, if it is a result of abuse, to follow relevant procedures.

It is important that she gets help and support as soon as possible. The doctor will need to assess Nadine's competence to consent to treatment and will make a judgement about whether or not Nadine can have an abortion without her parents' consent.

Some school policies will require that teachers tell the head teacher, who in turn tells the parents; others will view Nadine's situation as a child protection issue and you will be expected to use the Child Protection Procedure. Neither of these are good practice and they could cause unnecessary distress for Nadine.

Asaf

Best practice is having a policy that supports ALL young people's confidentiality and supports you in talking confidently and openly with Asaf. You will need to ascertain why he is telling you. It is not helpful to assume this is a problem for him. Best practice would be finding out:

- Why he has told you and what he hopes you will be able to offer him, i.e. does he want you to do anything?
- Are there any members of his family or any friends who can give him support?
- Does he need specific information and advice about sex or relationships? How will this be accessed?
- Are there specific gay and lesbian youth projects that he can access if he wants to?

It is not good practice to apply a different rule of confidentiality for gay and lesbian pupils than for heterosexual pupils.

Tasha

Best practice would mean having a policy that assures Tasha's confidentiality and an environment that does not perpetuate or collude with prejudice. This requires that all types of bullying and harassment be challenged within the whole-school environment. Tasha should be clear who knows about her HIV status and understand why they know.

Tasha is making a decision not to leave the classroom and therefore this needs to be respected. All pupils need to hear a strong message from the teacher that makes it clear that bullying and prejudice are not acceptable within the school and Tasha needs to be affirmed as a valid and valued individual.

It would be helpful to talk to Tasha discreetly either immediately at the end of the lesson or as soon as possible.

Resources list

The first section provides key government resources and documents. The second section offers resources published by the Sex Education Forum and relevant resources from David Fulton Publishers. The Sex Education Forum regularly updates resource lists including activity packs and videos. These lists are available on the website www.ncb.org.uk/sef or by phoning 020 7843 6056.

Key government documents and resources

Department for Education and Employment (2000) *Sex and Relationship Education Guidance* (0116/2000). London: DfEE.

Department for Education and Employment and Qualifications and Curriculum Authority (1999) *The National Curriculum Handbook for Secondary School Teachers in England*. London: DfEE.

Department for Education and Employment and Qualifications and Curriculum Authority (1999) *The National Curriculum Handbook for Primary School Teachers in England*. London: DfEE.

National Healthy School Standard (1999a) *Guidance*. London: DfEE.

National Healthy School Standard (1999b) *Getting Started*. London: Department of Health and Department for Education and Employment.

Qualifications and Curriculum Authority (2000a) *Personal, Social and Health Education and Citizenship at Key Stages One and Two: Initial Guidance*. London: QCA.

Qualifications and Curriculum Authority (2000b) *Personal, Social and Health Education at Key Stages Three and Four: Initial Guidance*. London: QCA.

Qualifications and Curriculum Authority (2000c) *Citizenship Education at Key Stages Three and Four: Initial Guidance*. London: QCA.

Social Exclusion Unit (1999) *Teenage Pregnancy*. London: HMSO.

Sex Education Forum resources

All of these resources are available from the National Children's Bureau tel. 020 7843 6000 or via the web bookshop www.ncb.org.uk

Blake, S. (2001) *Sex and Relationships Education Modules.* Bristol: Award Scheme Development Accreditation Network/Sex Education Forum and National Children's Bureau.

Blake, S. and Frances, G. (2001) *Just Say No! to Abstinence Education: Report of a Sex Education Study Tour to the United States.* London: Sex Education Forum/National Children's Bureau.

Blake, S. and Katrak, Z. (2002) *Faith, Values and Sex and Relationships Education.* London: Sex Education Forum.

Jolly, J. with Ray, C. and Thistle, S. (2002) *Relationships, Growing Up and Us! Developing Sex and Relationships Education in the Primary School.* London: Sex Education Forum.

Lenderyou, G. and Ray, C. (eds) (1997) *Let's Hear it for the Boys! Supporting Sex and Relationships Education for Boys and Young Men.* London: Sex Education Forum.

Patel-Kanwal, H. and Frances-Lenderyou, G. (1998) *Let's Talk about Sex and Relationships: A Policy and Practice Framework for Working with Children and Young People in Public Care.* London: Sex Education Forum.

Scott, L. (1996) *Partnership with Parents: A Guide for Schools and Those Working with Them.* London: Sex Education Forum.

Sex Education Forum (2002) *Sex, Relationships, Myths and Education: Young People's Views on SRE.* A video resource. London: Sex Education Forum/National Children's Bureau.

The Sex Education Forum produces a range of 4- and 8-page Forum Factsheets. They are designed to offer accessible and practical digests of current research and ideas. Each factsheet focuses on a specific aspect of SRE. For a full list of titles contact the Sex Education Forum on 020 7843 6056 or visit the website and download them for free www.ncb.org.uk/sexed.htm. Current titles include:

- *The Framework for Sex and Relationships Education* (1999).
- *Taking the Initiative: Positive Guidance on Sex and Relationships Education in the Secondary School (2000).*
- *Ensuring Entitlement: Sex and Relationships Education for Disabled Children (2001).*
- *PSHE and Citizenship: Ensuring Effective Sex and Relationships Education (2001).*
- *Sex and Relationships Education in the Primary School (2002).*

David Fulton publications

Fairburn, G., Rowley, D. and Bowen, M. (1995) *Sexuality, Learning Difficulties and Doing What's Right.* London: David Fulton. Addresses issues that arise in relation to the sexuality of people with learning difficulties. The authors use a storytelling approach to explore the rights of people with learning difficulties to be informed about sexuality, to form relationships, and to express their sexual nature. It is intended as an introduction to some of the aspects of the moral territory in which practical decisions are embedded.

McLaughlin, C. and Byers, R. (2001) *Personal and Social Development for All*. London: David Fulton. This book addresses the promotion of personal and social development for pupils with learning difficulties and considers the social context in which teaching and learning occur. The authors show how to implement effective record-keeping and evaluation, promote individual support and ensure pupils' smooth transition to adulthood.

Otten, L. (1999) *A Curriculum for Personal and Social Education*. London: David Fulton. Written by teachers from a secondary school for pupils with severe learning difficulties, this book provides a progressive health education curriculum for pupils with moderate and severe learning difficulties. Emphasis is placed on a whole-school approach to sex and health education that builds on existing skills. A suggested curriculum (including activities) is provided in the areas of substance misuse and abuse, sex education, family life education, personal safety, food and nutrition, personal hygiene, advocacy and independence and leisure.

An audit tool for reviewing sex and relationships education provision

Criteria	What's happening now?	What changes would you like to make?	How will progress be monitored?
The school has an up-to-date Sex and Relationships Education policy which has been developed in line with legal requirements and non-statutory guidance, and forms part of an overall PSHE and Citizenship policy.			
The school has established mechanisms for involving and consulting pupils, parents, staff, governors and the wider community in the development of the policy and practice, including sexual health and support services.			
The school has a clear confidentiality policy known to pupils, staff, parents and visitors.			
The school has a Sex and Relationships curriculum that fulfils statutory requirements and takes into account non-statutory guidance.			

Schools with secondary-aged pupils teach about HIV and STIs.					
There is a planned Sex and Relationships Education programme that has clear learning outcomes and is relevant to all different pupils, and promotes emotional resourcefulness and self-esteem. A range of teaching methods is used and a safe learning environment is established.					
Links are made between Sex and Relationships Education and other areas e.g. Science, English and RE.					
Pupil learning is monitored and assessed and this informs future planning.					
Staff have a sound basic knowledge of Sex and Relationships issues and are confident in their skills to teach and discuss these issues.					
Staff have an understanding of the role of schools in contributing to the reduction of teenage pregnancies and promotion of sexual health.					

This audit tool has been adapted from Camden and Islington Healthy Schools Scheme.

Glossary of terms

At the Sex Education Forum we often get asked for ways of explaining or describing particular activities or body parts. This glossary of terms is for workers who want to familiarise themselves with terms that are related to sex, sexuality and relationships.

Term	Definition
Areola	The area around the nipple.
Bisexual	A term used to describe men and women who are attracted to (and may have sex with) both the same and the opposite gender.
Celibate	When a person makes a reasoned decision to abstain from sexual activity.
Cervix	A ring of muscle closing the lower end of the uterus where it joins the vagina.
Clitoris	The female sex organ that produces feelings of pleasure when stimulated.
Ejaculation	When the sperm is released from the penis during orgasm.
Fallopian tube	The tube that runs from each ovary to the womb. This is the tube along which the ovum travels.
Female genital mutilation	FGM is illegal in Britain and is a child protection issue. It is a cultural tradition that is often assumed to have religious significance. There are three forms of female genital mutilation.
Fertilisation	When the reproductive cells (sperm and ovum) join together.
Foreskin	The thin skin that covers the end of the penis.

Gay (homosexual)	A term used for men and women who are attracted to (and may have sex with) the same gender.
Genitals	The sex organs of men and women.
Gonads	The sex glands which produce ova and sperm (the ovaries in women and the testicles in men).
Graafian follicle	The area in the ovary where the egg develops.
Heterosexual	The term for men and women who are attracted to (and may have sex with) someone of the opposite gender.
Homosexual	See Gay
Hormones	Chemical substances that are produced by glands which control the development of the body.
Implantation	When the fertilised ovum embeds into the lining of the uterus.
Intercourse –	
Anal	When the penis is put into the anus.
Vaginal	When the penis is put into the vagina.
Labia (inner and outer)/lips	The folds of skin that protect the opening of the vagina.
Labour	The process that leads up to the birth of a baby.
Lesbian	A term used for women who are attracted to (and may have sex with) women.
Male circumcision	The foreskin is removed soon after birth and this has religious significance for many faith communities including Muslims and Jews.
Oestrogen	A female sex hormone.
Oral sex	When a person kisses or licks another person's sexual organ (penis, vagina, testicles or clitoris).
Orgasm	A feeling of extreme pleasure at the climax of sexual activity.
Ovary (pl. ovaries)	The female reproductive organ(s) where ova are produced.
Ovulation	The release of a mature ovum from the ovary.
Ovum (pl. ova)	A female egg cell.

Penis	The male sex organ that becomes erect if a man is sexually excited and gives feelings of sexual excitement and pleasure if it is stimulated.
Periods	The breakdown of the lining of the womb. This happens approximately every 28 days. A small amount of blood is lost through the vagina.
Placenta	A structure that is formed between the embryo and the uterine lining. This enables the embryo to obtain food and oxygen from its mother's blood.
Progesterone	A female sex hormone.
Prostate gland	A gland which surrounds the neck of the bladder. The sperm cells are mixed with seminal fluid in the prostate gland.
Puberty	The period when the sex organs become active. It begins early in adolescence and ends when a young person is fully developed. Puberty happens at different ages and is marked by the growth of pubic hair, changes in the body shape, the development of breasts, etc.
Pubic bone	Front part of the pelvis immediately above the external sex organs.
Pubic hair	Hair around the external sex organs which begins to grow during puberty.
Scrotum	Sac that holds the testes outside the body.
Semen	The fluid that contains sperm and is ejaculated when a man has an orgasm.
Seminal fluid	The fluid that is produced by the seminal vesicles and protects the sperm as they swim inside the female body.
Seminal vesicles	The male sex glands that are situated behind the bladder which produce the seminal fluid.
Sperm	Male seed that is necessary to fertilise the ovum.
Testicles	Two male sex organs that produce sperm and male sex hormones.
Testis (pl. testes)	The medical name for the testicles.
Testosterone	A male sex hormone.
Umbilical cord	The tube that joins the foetus to the placenta.

Ureter	The tube that connects the kidney to the bladder. Urine passes through this tube.
Urethra	The tube through which urine travels from the bladder to the outside of the body.
Uterus	The female muscular organ in which the embryo develops.
Vagina	The passageway from the cervix to the outside of the body.
Vulva	The external female sex organs.
Wet dream	When a boy/man ejaculates in their sleep. This is common during puberty.
Womb	See Uterus.

Useful organisations

Black Health Agency
Zion Community Health and Resource Centre
339 Stretford Road
Hulme
Manchester
M15 4ZY
0161 226 9145
www. blackhealthagency.co.org.uk
Provides a range of health-related services and initiatives for the diverse Black communities locally, regionally and nationally.

Brook
Unit 421
Highgate Studios
52–79 Highgate Road
London NW5 1TL
020 7284 6040
www.brook.org.uk
Publishes a range of resources for young people and professionals.

Centre for HIV and Sexual Health
22 Collegiate Crescent
Sheffield
S10 2BA
0114 226 1900
www.sheffhiv.demon.co.uk
Offers training, consultancy and resources for children, young people and professionals.

Education for Choice
2–12 Pentonville Road
London N1 9FP
020 7837 7221
www.efc.org.uk
Provides materials and training for teachers and professionals working with young people on abortion and choice.

FPA
2–12 Pentonville Road
London N1 9FP
020 7837 5432
www.fpa.org.uk
Offers training and consultancy as well as resources for children, young people and professionals.

Health Development Agency
Holborn Gate
330 High Holborn
London WC1V 7BA
020 7430 0850
www.hda-online.org.uk
Offers research, support and resources. The National Healthy School Standard national team is based at the Health Development Agency.

Image in Action
Chinnor Road
Bledlow Bridge
High Wycombe
HP14 4AJ
01494 481 632
Image in Action works with young people with learning disabilities using drama, group work and active learning to teach sex education. Has produced two resources.

National Children's Bureau
8 Wakley Street
London EC1V 7QE
020 7843 6000
www.ncb.org.uk
Offers an information service and produces a range of resources, and offers training and consultancy on all aspects of PSHE and Citizenship.

Sex Education Forum
8 Wakley Street
London EC1V 7QE
020 7843 6056
www.ncb.org.uk/sexed.htm
Offers a range of publications and factsheets including *Sex Education Matters*, a termly newletter currently free of charge to all schools.

Working with Men
320 Commercial Way
London SE15 1QN
020 8308 0709
Training and resources for working with boys and young men.

References

Adams, J. (2002) *Go Girls! Supporting Emotional Development and Self-Esteem.* Sheffield: Centre for HIV and Sexual Health.

Blake, S. (1999) *Consultations with Young Heterosexual Men.* London: Health Education Authority.

Blake, S. (2001) *Sex and Relationships Education Modules.* Bristol: ASDAN/Sex Education Forum/National Children's Bureau.

Blake, S. and Frances, G. (2001) *Just Say No! to Abstinence Education: Report of a Sex Education Study Tour to the United States.* London: Sex Education Forum/National Children's Bureau.

Blake, S., Hilton, R. and Owen, C. (2001) *Included or Excluded: SRE in Pupil Referral Units.* London: Sex Education Matters 24: 9 and 10.

Blake, S. and Katrak, Z. (2002) *Faith, Values and Sex and Relationships Education.* London: Sex Education Forum.

Blake, S. and Laxton, J. (1998) *STRIDES: A Practical Guide to Sex and Relationships Education with Young Men.* London: FPA.

Buston, K. and Wight, D. (2002) 'The Salience of Sex Education in Young Women's Lives'. *Sex Education,* vol. 2, no. 3.

Children and Young People's Unit (2000) *Learning to Listen: Core Principles for Involving Children and Young People.* London: The Stationery Office.

Collyer, J. (1995) *Sex Education in the Primary Schools: A Guide to Policy Development in Primary Schools.* London: Forbes.

Commission for Racial Equality (2001) *Statutory Code of Practice on the Duty to Promote Racial Equality: A Guide for Schools. Consultation Draft.* London: Commission for Racial Equality.

Cross, S. (2000) *Can I Catch it from a Toothbrush? Children calling Childine about HIV and AIDS.* London: Childline.

Department for Education and Employment (1994) *Sex Education in Schools.* London: HMSO.

Department for Education and Employment (1999) *Social Inclusion: Pupil Support 11/99.* London: HMSO.

Department for Education and Employment (2000) *Sex and Relationship Education Guidance (0116/2000).* London: DfEE.

Dix, D. (1996) *Sex Education for Parents: A Resource Pack for Professionals.* Cardiff: Health Promotion Wales/FPA Cymru.

Eales, J. and Watson, J. (1994) *Health Education in Scottish Schools: Meeting Special Educational Needs.* Scottish Office.

Forrest, S., Biddle, G. and Clift, S. (1997) *Talking about Homosexuality in the Secondary School.* Horsham: AVERT.

Forum on Children and Violence (2001) *A Young People's Charter for a Non-Violent Society.* London: Forum on Children and Violence.

Frosh, S., Phoenix, A. and Pattman, R. (2001) *Young Masculinities: Understanding Boys in Contemporary Society.* Oxford: Palgrave.

Health Development Agency (2001) *Key Characteristics of Interventions Designed to Reduce Teenage Pregnancy: An Update.* London: Health Development Agency.

Health Education Authority (1996) *Is Video an Effective Tool for Health Education? Health Promotion Effectiveness Reviews, Summary Bulletin 3.* London: Health Education Authority.

Health Education Authority/National Foundation for Educational Research (1994) *Parents, Schools and Sex Education – A Compelling Case for Partnership.* London: Health Education Authority/National Foundation for Educational Research.

Holland, J. (1993) *Sexuality and Ethnicity: Variations in Young Women's Sexual Knowledge and Practice.* WRAP Paper 8. London: Tufnell Press.

Holland, J., Ramazanoglu, C. and Sharpe, S. (1993) *Wimp or Gladiator: Contradictions in Acquiring Masculine Sexuality.* WRAP/MRAP Paper 9. London: Tufnell Press.

Holland, J., Ramazanoglu, C., Sharpe, S. and Thomson, R. (1998) *The Male in the Head: Young People, Heterosexuality and Power.* London: Tufnell Press.

Hunter, J., Phillips, S. and Whetton, N. (1998) *Hand in Hand: Emotional Development through Literature.* London: Saffire Press.

Ingham, R. (1998) 'Exploring Interactional Competence: Comparative Data from the United Kingdom and the Netherlands on Young People's Sexual Development'. Paper presented at the 24th meeting of the International Academy of Sex Research, Sirmione, Italy.

Ingham, R. (2002) 'Young People, Alcohol and Sexual Conduct'. Paper presented to the Sex Education Forum and Drug Education Forum – Drugs, alcohol and sexual risk-taking seminar. London: Institute of Education.

Johns, R., Scott, L. and Bliss J. (1997) *Let's Do It: Creative Activities for Sex Education with Young People with Learning Difficulties.* London: Image in Action.

Jolly, J. with Ray, C. and Thistle, S. (2002) *Relationships, Growing Up and Us! Developing Sex and Relationships Education in the Primary School.* London: Sex Education Forum.

Kirby, D. (1995) 'Editorial'. *British Medical Journal,* vol. 311, no. 7002, p. 403.

Kline, N. (1998) *Time to Think.* London: Ward Lock.

Lees, J. and Plant, S. (2001) *PASSPORT: A Framework for Personal and Social Development.* London: Calouste Gulbenkian Foundation.

Lenderyou, G. and Ray, C. (eds) (1997) *Let's Hear it for the Boys: Supporting Sex and Relationships Education with Boys and Young Men.* London: Sex Education Forum.

Lewis, L. (2001) *Afraid to Say: The Needs and Views of Children and Young People Living with HIV/AIDS.* London: National Children's Bureau/Strutton Housing.

Mason, A. and Palmer, A. (1996) *Queerbashing: A Survey of Hate Crimes against Gay Men and Lesbians.* London: Stonewall.

National Healthy School Standard (1999a) *Guidance*. London: Department for Education and Employment and Department of Health.

National Healthy School Standard (1999b) *Getting Started: A Guide for Schools*. London: Department for Education and Employment and Department of Health.

National Healthy School Standard (2001) *Sex and Relationships Education*. London: Department for Education and Employment/Department of Health.

Office for National Statistics (1999) *Population Trends 1999*. London: ONS.

Office for Standards in Education (2002) *Sex and Relationships Education in Schools*. Norwich: The Stationery Office.

Patel-Kanwal, H. and Frances-Lenderyou, G. (1998) *Let's Talk about Sex and Relationships*. London: Sex Education Forum.

Prendergast, F. (1994) *This is the Time to Grow Up: Girl's Experiences of Menstruation in Schools*. London: Family Planning Association.

Public Health Laboratory Service. Sexually Transmitted Infections in the UK: New episodes seen at G.U.M. clinics 1995–2000. www.phls.co.uk/facts/sti/files

Qualifications and Curriculum Authority/DfEE (1999) *The National Curriculum Handbook for Primary Schools*. London: QCA/DfEE.

Qualifications and Curriculum Authority (2000) *Personal, Social and Health Education at Key Stages 3 and 4: Initial Guidance in Schools*. London: QCA.

Ray, C. (2000) *Meeting the Needs of Girls and Young Women in Sex and Relationships Education*. London: Sex Education Forum.

Rogers, M. (1994) 'Growing up lesbian' in Epstein, D. (ed.) *Challenging Lesbian and Gay Inequalities in Education*. Buckingham: Open University Press.

Schutz, W. (1965) *The Interpersonal Underworld*. London: Science and Behaviour Books.

Scott, L. (1996) *Partnership with Parents*. London: Sex Education Forum.

Sex Education Forum (1999) *The Framework for Sex and Relationships Education*. London: Sex Education Forum.

Sex Education Forum (2000) *Our (Young People) Charter for Good Sex and Relationships Education*. London: Sex Education Forum.

Sex Education Forum (2001) *PSHE and Citizenship: Ensuring Effective Sex and Relationships Education*. London: Sex Education Forum.

Social Exclusion Unit (1999) *Teenage Pregnancy*. London: HMSO.

Thomson, A. and Scott, S. (1991) *Learning about Sex: Young Women and the Social Constitution of Sexual Identity*. WRAP Paper. London: Tufnell Press.

Tuckman, B. (1965) 'Sequences in small groups'. *Psychological Bulletin*, vol. 6, pp. 384–9.

Wight, D., Henderson, M., Raab, G., Abraham, C., Buston, K., Scott, S. and Hart, G. (2000) 'Extent of regretted sexual intercourse among young teenagers in Scotland: a cross-sectional survey'. *British Medical Journal*, vol. 320, pp. 1243–4.

Wild, G. (1997) 'Supporting sex and relationships education in primary schools' in Lenderyou, G. and Ray, C. *Let's Hear it for the Boys: Supporting Sex and Relationships Education for Boys and Young Men*. London: Sex Education Forum.

Index

personal experience 36, 99
personality, teacher's 48
planning 13, 21–3, 45–6, 83–4, 87–91,
   98–100
policy 7, 13–16, 18–20, 62, 73, 83, 98, 110
posters 46, 47, 51
practical skills 33
practicing 32
pregnancy 8, 9, 18, 20, 27–8, 111, 114
Preston Youth Forum 45
Primary Care Group/Trust 18, 20, 39
primary pupils with severe learning
   difficulties 87–9
primary school 7, 21, 61–70, 112
problem-solving skills 34
professional development 48–9, 105–15
puberty 54, 62, 66–7
public and private 86–90
pupil assessment 52–3
Pupil Referral Units (PRUs) 7, 95–103
puppets 70

Qualifications and Curriculum
   Authority 21, 97
Quality Protects 44
questionnaires 41
questions 39, 51
quizzes 41

Race Relations Amendment Act (2000)
   57
'real-life scenarios
   and professional development
      112–14
   using 21
Redbridge LEA 46
reflection 32, 38
reinforcement 38, 83
relationships 87–90
Religious Education 23
repetition 38, 83
reporting 50
reporting back 40
reproduction 67–8, 69
resources 18, 23–5, 83, 117–19

review 16–17
   audit for 121–2
rituals 37, 83, 100
role model
   teacher as 49, 60, 99
   visitors as 102–3
role-play 42
Rotherham Primary Care Trust 20
Rowley, D. 118–19
SMT (Senior Management Team) 12
SRE *Guidance* see *Sex and Relationships
   Education Guidance*
STIs 30
safer sex 77, 87
safety 43
St Luke's Special School, Hertfordshire
   52
school councils 45
school culture 43–6
school nurses 27, 62
school nursing profiles 18, 20
Science (National Curriculum) 7, 64,
   67–8, 74
secondary pupils with severe learning
   difficulties 89–90
secondary school 7, 12, 21, 71–80,
   113–14
self-assessment 105–6
self-esteem 4, 30
self-reflection 51–2, 108–10
Senior Management Team (SMT) 12
services 23, 39, 46–7, 79–80
severe learning disabilities 87–91, 92
*Sex and Relationships Education
   Guidance (SRE Guidance)* (DfEE) 6, 7,
      13, 17, 18, 24, 46, 49, 64, 74, 79
Sex Education Forum vi, 1, 3, 19, 23, 24,
   28, 44, 45, 48, 50, 70, 78, 95, 97, 109,
   118
sexual health 8–9
   services 23, 39, 46–7, 79–80
sexual intercourse 8, 68
sexually abused children/young people
   59–60
Sheffield Sexual Health Forum 25, 28